OECD INSIGHTS

Sustainable Development

Linking economy, society, environment

By Tracey Strange and Anne Bayley

ORGANISATION FOR ECONOMIC CO-OPERATION AND DEVELOPMENT

The OECD is a unique forum where the governments of 30 democracies work together to address the economic, social and environmental challenges of globalisation. The OECD is also at the forefront of efforts to understand and to help governments respond to new developments and concerns, such as corporate governance, the information economy and the challenges of an ageing population. The Organisation provides a setting where governments can compare policy experiences, seek answers to common problems, identify good practice and work to co-ordinate domestic and international policies.

The OECD member countries are: Australia, Austria, Belgium, Canada, the Czech Republic, Denmark, Finland, France, Germany, Greece, Hungary, Iceland, Ireland, Italy, Japan, Korea, Luxembourg, Mexico, the Netherlands, New Zealand, Norway, Poland, Portugal, the Slovak Republic, Spain, Sweden, Switzerland, Turkey, the United Kingdom and the United States. The Commission of the European Communities takes part in the work of the OECD.

OECD Publishing disseminates widely the results of the Organisation's statistics gathering and research on economic, social and environmental issues, as well as the conventions, guidelines and standards agreed by its members.

This work is published on the responsibility of the Secretary-General of the OECD. The opinions expressed and arguments employed herein do not necessarily reflect the official views of the Organisation or of the governments of its member countries.

Also available in French under the title:

Les essentiels de l'OCDE
Le développement durable

Foreword

Since the Brundtland Commission published its landmark report in 1987, we have come a long way in our reflections on sustainable development. Few would dispute its fundamental principles: that our actions must take into account effects on the environment, economy and society, and that what we do today should not compromise the well-being of future generations.

In the last 20 years, significant progress has been made. Most national governments have begun to incorporate sustainable development into their planning and policy. Pro-active businesses across the globe have brought sustainability to their products and processes. Local initiatives have had success in informing citizens of the importance of participating in reducing waste, renewing urban spaces and other programs.

In spite of these efforts, though, putting the principles of sustainable development into practice has proven to be anything but simple or straightforward. After all, both people and institutions have their habits, and changing them, even when the need is obvious, can be daunting. A key question remains whether we have made enough progress, or taken the warnings seriously enough to allow us to grasp and confront our biggest, most pressing problems.

We have solid evidence of climate change, with projections pointing to an increase in extreme environmental events with potentially devastating consequences for the systems that support human life and society. About half the world still lives on less than $2.50 dollars a day, lacks access to clean water, sanitation, adequate health care and education – an unacceptably stark contrast to the much higher standards of living in developed countries. Some emerging economies, such as China and India, are undergoing rapid growth, resulting in more wealth, but also an increased demand for energy and greater pollution problems. Finding sustainable solutions for growth holds the potential to help reduce poverty, foster development and preserve the environment. Implementing them requires political will and co-operation on a global scale.

The OECD has been at the forefront of the effort to advance sustainable development. We have supported extensive research on the challenges of sustainability and been active in efforts to develop best practices in areas such as sustainable production and consumption and measuring sustainable development. One of the significant challenges lies in policy coherence – ensuring that different policies and practices support each other in reaching a goal. Achieving this coherence in our policies and institutions is essential to achieving real and lasting progress. With a long record of research, analysis and international co-operation, the OECD can offer policy options for addressing these challenges.

The aim of the *Insights* series is to generate an informed debate on some of the key issues that affect our societies and economies today. For a truly meaningful dialogue, we need to go beyond exchanging opinions – no matter how fiercely they are held – and look at the facts and figures. We also need to move beyond jargon. After all, it is this kind of inclusive and broad-based dialogue that will produce the most widely-supported decisions and strongest results.

Angel Gurría
Secretary-General of the OECD

Acknowledgements

The authors gratefully acknowledge the editorial contribution from Patrick Love and the substantive input and advice from the following:

Nick Bray, Emmanuel Dalmenesche, Adeline Destombes, Jeremy Hurst, Enrico Giovannini, Brian Keeley, Kumi Kitamori, Katherine Kraig-Ernandes, Vincent Koen, Raili Lahnalampi, Wilfrid Legg, Lorents Lorentsen, Marco Mira d'Ercole, Thorvald Moe, Helen Mountford, Christoph Müller, Mario Pezzini, Candice Stevens, Ton Boon von Ochssee.

Currency Note

Currency references are in US dollars unless otherwise indicated.

This book has...

StatLinkS

A service from OECD Publishing that delivers Excel™ files from the printed page!

Look for the *StatLinks* at the bottom right-hand corner of the tables or graphs in this book. To download the matching Excel™ spreadsheet, just type the link into your internet browser, starting with the *http://dx.doi.org* prefix.
If you're reading the PDF e-book edition, and your pc is connected to the Internet, simply click on the link. You'll find *StatLinks* appearing in more OECD books.

CONTENTS

1

Life depends on a complex set of interactions between people, the natural environment and economic systems. The unprecedented growth seen during the 20th century has affected these relationships in both positive and negative ways. Record levels of pollution have put great stress on the environment. Economic growth has created immense wealth in some areas of the globe, but left others behind. Understanding the essential elements that support healthy societies and a healthy planet is an urgent need for people and their governments.

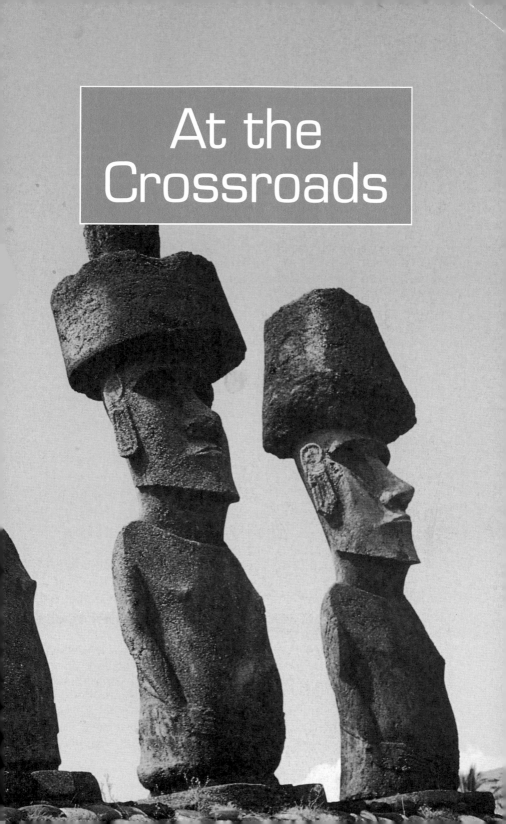

At the Crossroads

By way of introduction...

Two thousand three hundred miles to the west of Chile and 1 300 miles to the east of Polynesia's Pitcairn Islands lies an island that has inspired intense interest for centuries, not for its perfect climate or its untouched beauty, but because it holds a secret, a mystery. Rapa Nui, or Easter Island as it was named by 18th century Dutch explorers, attracts scientists from around the world who come to study its stone statues, called moai.

The moai, like the pyramids of ancient Egypt, intrigue and confound us with their sheer size: weighing up to 270 tonnes and as much as 70 feet tall, these massive monolithic figures form an imposing presence: outsized human faces looking out over this remote island and the thousands of miles of ocean that lie beyond it. We marvel at the engineering and wonder at how stone-age Polynesians managed to erect such immense structures without the use of cranes, metal tools, or large animals. The creation of statuary of this size and sophistication speaks to the existence of a populous, creative and complex society – one that was well-off enough to support an artisan class. They could afford to allocate time and resources to the various activities involved in making, transporting and erecting hundreds of statues.

Or could they? European explorers who visited the island in the 18th and 19th centuries found a population of only a few thousand, a mere remnant of the statue-building society that came before. Something had significantly altered life on Rapa Nui.

What had at one time been a sub-tropical forest was now a completely deforested island, with at least 22 species of trees and plants extinct. Most wild sources of food were gone – overhunting had left Easter with almost no wild bird species. Without trees to make canoes, large fish were inaccessible, leaving only fish that could be caught close to shore. Evidence shows that these stocks too were depleted. What happened to bring Easter's civilisation to near extinction, driving its population almost to zero and ending its period of cultural flourishing and creative production? In his book *Collapse*, Jared Diamond suggests a scenario in which the population continued to exploit resources available to them beyond their limits, in an environment whose ecological fragility made it vulnerable to permanent destruction. The exact cause of the deforestation is still being debated. The trees were cut to supply wood for rollers and beams to transport the statues. Forest was cleared for agriculture. Trees were also burned to obtain charcoal.

Another possibility is that rats brought to the island by the first settlers fed off the seeds of the trees. Easter's collapse has inspired thousands of pages of study and analysis – in part because islands make interesting cases studies, providing a kind of closed Petri dish in which we can study cause and effect. But Easter also intrigues us because of the extent of its devastation, what Diamond calls "the most extreme example of forest destruction in the Pacific, and among the most extreme in the world." Is there a lesson in this experience for the world of today? What can we learn from Easter's cautionary tale?

The relationship of humans to the environment has always been one of give and take. Easter Islanders made use of their surroundings for their physical and cultural needs in the same way that all human societies do – but they either did not see or did not heed the requirement of keeping their "systems" in balance, of ensuring that new trees were growing when old trees were cut, for example. When the rate of use overtakes the rate at which a resource can be replenished, then that resource will be drawn down and eventually disappear, affecting all of the people, animals and plants that depend on it.

The question of equilibrium – balancing use with renewal, pollution with its impact on ecosystems – is key to understanding the challenges of our world. Even CO_2 emissions that we all worry about these days serve a beneficial purpose, being absorbed by plants for increased growth, as long as the proportions remain right: the carbon dioxide put into the atmosphere should not exceed what can be absorbed through photosynthesis. Problems arise when proportions get out of balance, such as with excessive CO_2 emissions that cannot be absorbed by the ocean, plants and other so-called carbon sinks, and thus contribute to climate change.

Keeping systems in balance is an important idea that reaches beyond environmental concerns. Think of the demographic balances in a given society, the interplay between births, deaths, emigration and immigration. For our economies, we must have enough young workers to replace retirees, and to fund their pensions. Finally, can societies remain stable when resources are concentrated in the hands of a few, while others go without?

"World population is projected to increase [by around 2 billion] by 2050. Practically all that growth will be in the developing countries of Asia and Africa. This will put increased strain on resources and systems that are already insufficient in many cases."

Emerging Risks in the 21st Century: An Agenda for Action

▶ This chapter starts by looking at the state of the world today. It describes the material progress the industrial era has brought and what this means for our daily lives. It then describes the downside – the social and economic inequalities and negative environmental impacts. Finally, it looks at where we are heading and the questions we should be asking about the sustainability of our societies.

How are we doing?

To look at the statistics, the world today is, on average, a prosperous place. Growth in the second half of the 20th century was greater than at any previous historical period. Average incomes have increased eightfold since 1820, while population is five times higher.

"The world economy performed better in the last half century than at any time in the past. World GDP increased six-fold from 1950 to 1998 with an average growth of 3.9 per cent a year compared with 1.6 from 1820 to 1950, and 0.3 per cent from 1500 to 1820."

The World Economy: A Millennial Perspective

Global life expectancy at birth in 1800 was about 30 years, compared with 67 in 2000 and 75 in the rich countries. In countries with well-developed health care systems, infant mortality has been brought to very low levels and vaccines have virtually eliminated life-threatening childhood diseases.

We also live in a period of intense cultural production and technical ability. The so-called information age has put virtually limitless amounts of data at our fingertips – provided that we have access to the technology that links us to it. Films, plays, books, music, scientific studies, analysis and opinion on everything from politics to sport are all readily available, creating the possibilities for a society that is better informed and more aware than in any previous historical epoch.

And we are not just learning or consuming all of this content as individuals – we are discussing it, interacting with it and refining it collaboratively. Blogs, wikis, website discussion threads: these have created a new nexus of information between "official" and "unofficial" communications. Some bloggers become authorities on their topics and influence trends. Wiki contributors become widely read. The lines of communication have essentially opened up, giving us the opportunity and the responsibility of understanding what is going on around us – provided that we learn to use all of this information in a meaningful way.

Indeed, our choices have multiplied in nearly every domain: educational, professional and personal. As students we can choose from hundreds of subjects of study and among an increasing number of educational institutions offering diplomas. Programmes like the EU's Erasmus exchange scheme encourage students from one country to study in another – to learn another language, another culture, or simply to have access to a particular type of education not available in their home country.

The globalisation of business, science and culture has also opened up our professional choices: following a job far from one's home town, working as an expatriate in another country, travelling regularly to offices around the world. On the whole, we are a wealthier, longer living, more educated and more mobile population. But can this continue? Will it be true for future generations? In all parts of the world?

Clouds on the horizon?

> "If everyone used energy and resources the same way we do in the Western World, we would need three more earths at least. And we have only one."
>
> Mona Sahlin, former Minister for Sustainable Development, Sweden,
> *Institutionalising Sustainable Development*

Still, in spite of the advanced state of many contemporary societies, we see some troubling contradictions. Notably, there is a stark inequality between those with access to the fruits of advanced development, and those living in contexts where that advancement is impeded by lack of access to what others take for granted.

Stark differences divide the world in terms of access to water and sanitation, energy, health care and education. For example, it is estimated that 1.1 billion people in the world lack clean water. The question is not one of comfort: water-related illnesses are the second biggest killer of children in the world – approximately 1.8 million children die each year from diseases caused by dirty water and poor sanitation. Illness from poor water and sanitation keeps children out of school and adults out of work, while the search for water in areas where access is poor takes up a large portion of time in the daily lives of women and girls, time that they cannot spend working for economic improvement or going to school.

According to the United Nations Human Development report and to water specialists like Professor A.K. Biswas, the problem is not one of scarcity, but mismanagement. Leaking taps in the developed world waste more water than is available to the billion people in the developing world who need it. Fixing those leaking taps won't magically solve water access problems, but an approach to water management that includes sharing successful techniques for making the best use of available water supplies can improve things dramatically.

While people living in the least developed nations often lack the necessary elements to fulfil basic needs and have access to a life of health and quality, the developed world suffers from having too much. Poorer countries face the terrible consequences of largely preventable diseases like malaria or AIDS, while the richer ones battles epidemics of excess, such as adult-onset (or Type II) diabetes and heart disease caused by obesity. There is a level of international co-operation never before seen in history bilaterally, or between governments, and multilaterally through institutions like the United Nations, OECD, World Bank and others. And yet there are still violent conflicts that place those caught in them in conditions of extreme insecurity and vulnerability. The human population continues to grow. Predictions have the current population of 6.5 billion increasing to over 8 billion by 2050. More and more of those people are living in cities, and everyone who has the means is using more resources. Our lives are full of more and more things. The proliferation of markets, products, and the ease of trade means that both our choices for consumption and the consequences of that increased activity are greater than ever.

Economic development has allowed for advances that have fundamentally changed the ways humans live from previous centuries, but these activities have also brought about problems with potentially dramatic consequences. Climate change is the most visible, most talked about at the moment, especially after the recent (2007) Intergovernmental Panel on Climate Change report confirmed that the climate is almost certainly undergoing significant change as a result of human activity. But economic development has also brought social challenges: countries are advancing at different speeds, and people within countries are living with vastly different quality of life. In many countries the gap between the rich and the poor is increasing rather than shrinking with economic growth.

Climate change is symbolic of the larger problem – one that is both practical and philosophical – of the dangers inherent in pushing our ecosystems out of balance. Are we pushing our societies and environment too far, too fast? Are we outrunning the regenerative possibilities inherent to our ecosystems? Are we creating social imbalances that cannot be corrected? Could we be on some kind of crash course, like the Easter Islanders, without even realising it?

> **"The loss of key elements of an ecosystem can alter the balance between its components and lead to long-term or permanent changes."**
> *Preserving Biodiversity and Promoting Biosafety* (an OECD Policy Brief)

When systems work, when they are in equilibrium, they tend to continually produce possibilities for renewal: if land is well-managed, given time to lie fallow and regenerate nutrients, then it continues to be fertile indefinitely. If not, then the quality of soil degrades and in some cases becomes useless. Wild species naturally replace themselves. But populations will crash, possibly to extinction, if they are overharvested.

We can even extend this notion to humans and their interactions. Children who are well-nourished, educated and cared for tend to flourish, carrying with them a lifelong capacity to contribute to their community. Deprive them of those things and the outcome is likely to be quite different. The same is true at the societal and governmental level. Abuse, conflict or deprivation can cause entire communities to collapse.

This can be applied to economic systems or markets. Imbalances in supply and demand, in savings and spending, in loans and investment can lead to economic crashes, recessions and depressions. The most talented economists are still unable to predict reliably when and why these events might occur, due to the extreme complexity of the world's economy. What we do know is that economic, environmental and social systems must all be kept in relative equilibrium, and also balanced with each other, to be sustainable.

One problem is that we do not know when the "critical threshold" of these systems will be reached and exceeded. To continue moving towards, even beyond these thresholds, is to take a great risk: are we creating a future that will experience failures of Earth's life-sustaining systems with increasing frequency and unpredictability? Are we living in a present where economic and social developments benefit some and leave others mired in need and conflict?

Where are we headed?

In the last 200 years, the world's economy has grown sixfold, and almost tenfold in the regions that were first to industrialise. Standards of living, health and education have improved considerably. At the same time, burning coal for energy led to deadly smog in England and the US, water pollution left entire lakes "dead", irrigation for cotton brought the Aral Sea to a fraction of its historical area, and now fossil fuel use is causing changes to our climate. In addition, economic and technological development has left huge gaps in prosperity, opportunity and standards of living. The question is: can we do a better job with development, starting now?

What are the principles driving these phenomena? What kind of future are they spelling out for our descendents? As we develop economically and socially, whether as individuals, governments or businesses, we need guiding principles that will help us make the right choices.

> **"Unsustainable development has degraded and polluted the environment in such a way that it acts now as the major constraint followed by social inequity that limits the implementation of perpetual growth."**
>
> Emil Salim, *Institutionalising Sustainable Development*

But do we really have to choose between progress and sound management of the systems that support us? Every day, we hear about new technologies that can benefit people, economy *and* the environment: public health programmes that improve health outcomes for more people, energy efficient alternatives for many of the products and processes we have come to rely on, and new non-toxic and durable materials.

If the Easter Islanders were aware of their dwindling resource base, history shows that they didn't take the necessary steps to prevent passing the critical threshold. Many people today realise that our world also shows signs of stress – and at the very least presents some core problems to which we need to find solutions. Evidence suggests that we need better ways of managing our natural resources; better ways of securing what people need to develop; better ways of co-ordinating our actions to take care of all the things we rely on to survive, thrive and prosper.

It is time to learn how to develop without these negative social and environmental side effects, and in a way that benefits more of us. Easter Island was isolated from trade and limited in its ecological resources; perhaps the only way its human residents could have prevented tragedy was through careful planning. We are living on a much larger scale, but could the same be true of us?

What this book is about...

No one knows what the future will look like. Good or bad, clean or dirty, peaceful or war-torn – what will we be able to achieve with the tools at our disposal? Technological progress has made many things possible, but there are signs that we are reaching some thresholds at which negative consequences can become more than just an inconvenience.

Growing awareness of the fragility of our world has caused us to look more seriously for solutions, not just to one-time problems, but to faulty approaches to development that are short-sighted and self-destructive. Scientists, politicians and citizens from every walk of life have informed this discussion, seeking ways of balancing the benefits of growth with the drawbacks it can produce if not done carefully and intelligently.

"The future of mankind is being shaped by issues that no one nation can address alone. Multilateral co-operation is instrumental in meeting the key challenges of this new world." – Angel Gurría, "Making the Most of Globalisation: The OECD and the MENA countries".

We do actually have the tools and information to plan our development *sustainably* – in a way that takes all aspects of development into account and prefers choices that maintain a maximum level of well-being over the long term. Identifying the most significant issues and making the necessary changes is anything but simple. **Sustainable development** provides a way of doing this: assessing our current situation, setting goals that will produce better results and making the right choices about the direction we want to take.

Chapter 2 explores the concept of sustainable development, its history and what it means to us today.

Chapter 3 looks at the global dimension of sustainable development and how we can put rich, poor and rapidly emerging economies on a sustainable path.

Chapter 4 explains the importance of planning for the future, managing our economic, human and natural resources so that we can continue improving our societies without leaving a messy legacy for years to come.

Chapter 5 looks at how we behave as producers and consumers and the critical role this plays in achieving sustainable development goals.

Chapter 6 shows us how we can measure the different aspects of sustainable development and why this is important.

Chapter 7 examines how governments and civil society work together in creating the incentives, rules and regulations that make sustainable development possible.

What is OECD?

The Organisation for Economic Co-operation and Development, or OECD, brings together the governments of countries committed to democracy and the market economy to tackle key economic, social and governance challenges in the globalised world economy. It has 30 member countries, the economies of which account for 68% of the world's trade and 78% of the world's Gross National Income, or GNI (a measure of countries' economic performance).

The OECD traces its roots back to the Marshall Plan that rebuilt Europe after World War II. The mission then was to work towards sustainable economic growth and employment and to raise people's living standards. These remain core goals of the OECD. The organisation also works to build sound economic growth, both for member countries and those in the developing world, and seeks to help the development of non-discriminatory global trade. With that in mind, the OECD has forged links with many of the world's emerging economies and shares expertise and exchanges views with more than 100 other countries and economies around the world.

In recent years, OECD has also begun a process of enlargement, inviting five other countries (Chile, Estonia, Israel, Russia and Slovenia) to open talks on joining the organisation, and offering enhanced engagement to five emerging economies (Brazil, China, India, Indonesia and South Africa).

Numbers are at the heart of the OECD's work. It is one of the world's leading sources for comparable data on subjects ranging from economic indicators to education and health. This data plays a key role in helping member governments to compare their policy experiences.

The OECD also produces guidelines, recommendations and templates for international co-operation on areas such as taxation and technical issues that are essential for countries to make progress in the globalising economy.
www.oecd.org.

OECD and sustainable development

OECD Ministers recognise that sustainable development is an overarching goal for their governments and the Organisation itself, and member countries bear a special responsibility in achieving sustainable development worldwide. Activities linked to sustainable development are overseen by the Annual Meeting of Sustainable Development Experts (AMSDE), government delegates from capitals who co-ordinate special projects as well as review progress in mainstreaming sustainable development concepts into the overall work of the OECD.

Many activities relate to sustainable development, from climate change analysis to development co-operation to corporate social responsibility. On this website, there are links to a wealth of projects and information which shed light on certain dimensions of the issues:
www.oecd.org/sustainabledevelopment.

2

It is impossible to know precisely what the consequences of unchecked or badly managed development will be, but we have enough information to understand that they are potentially negative, costly and irreversible. Sustainable development gives us a new way of thinking through and managing human impact on the world – one that can generate long-lasting positive results for the greater benefit of human societies.

What is Sustainable Development?

By way of introduction...

Monique Huteau, a recently retired nurse, is up to her elbows in soil as she tends to her lush garden. Strawberries, lettuce, squash, potatoes and more, she grows enough to cover a large portion of her family's needs in produce, buying what she lacks at the local hypermart. She also cooks, cleans, cares for her grandchildren and paints watercolours at her home in the countryside a few minutes outside Poitiers, France.

During their working years, she and most of her nine siblings earned considerably more than their parents had, poor farmers from the Anjou region. They live in well-maintained houses, drive nice cars, and take yearly vacations to distant places. A lot of hard work and astute savings and investments have allowed Monique and her husband, a retired teacher, to achieve these things – with the help of French social benefits which have kept their health care and education costs low and ensured them an adequate retirement income. For Monique there is no question: her generation had opportunities not available to their parents and consequently live very different lives materially and socially.

Monique's experience is a common one in OECD countries: generations that had endured scarcity and hardship growing up have achieved, even on relatively modest incomes, the satisfaction of basic needs plus enough discretionary income to indulge in a few luxuries. With this have also come certain social benefits. Education levels have increased. More people have access to health care. Leisure time is guaranteed through paid vacations and retirement plans. There is more geographic and social mobility.

Indeed, the so-called developed world has seen average improvements in many areas that are important to "the good life". Along with these improvements, however, have come worrying indications that this growth has costs which we cannot continue to ignore.

All the economic prosperity in the world cannot alone solve a problem like climate change on its own. On the contrary, unchecked growth – in the number of people driving cars and taking planes, for example – is making the situation worse. Also, average economic growth says nothing about income inequality: if wealth is growing for only a few, then the majority may not experience any tangible gains or improvements.

These problems are compounded when added to the challenges facing the developing world – encompassing countries such as China and India who are undergoing rapid growth, as well as those like many Sub-Saharan African countries which are still far from having what the richer countries take for granted: peace, basic health care access, education, a relatively safe water supply, and so on.

Finally, do the resources exist to enable this kind of lifestyle for all of Earth's 6.5 billion residents? It is estimated that in 2002 humans extracted over 50 billion tons of natural resources from the planet's ecosystems, up a third in just 20 years. Projected economic growth rates put our extraction needs at 80 billion tons in 2020. Would using the Earth's resources at this rate be advisable? Can we and should we continue with the traditional model of development?

These problems are not new. Indeed, the accumulation of a number of bad habits and "unsustainable" practices seems to have led to critical stresses on societies and the environment. In spite of unprecedented economic growth, the world has been on a course leading to resource depletion and serious social crises, and old ways of problem-solving have proven inadequate. Something has to be done to change development – its philosophy and methods – if societies wanted to reverse those negative trends. As Albert Einstein wrote, "Today's problems cannot be solved if we still think the way we thought when we created them."

▶ We hear the term "sustainable development" in high-level discussions; we see it in political platforms and on corporate websites. More and more universities have programmes covering the field. Indeed, sustainable development has become a kind of conceptual touchstone, one of the defining ideas of contemporary society. This chapter reviews the debate on what exactly the concept of sustainable development means. It looks at where the term came from and what it now includes. And it asks how we can make use of the concept in our daily lives and our systems of governance.

Defining sustainable development

Development: the act or process of developing; growth; progress.

Sustainable development: development that meets the needs of the present without compromising the ability of future generations to meet their own needs.

The term sustainable development began to gain wide acceptance in the late 1980s, after its appearance in *Our Common Future*, also known as *The Brundtland Report*. The result of a UN-convened commission created to propose "a global agenda for change" in the concept and practices of development, the Brundtland report signalled the urgency of re-thinking our ways of living and governing. To "responsibly meet humanity's goals and aspirations" would require new ways of considering old problems as well as international co-operation and co-ordination.

The World Commission on Environment and Development, as it was formally called, sought to draw the world's attention to "the accelerating deterioration of the human environment and natural resources and the consequences of that deterioration for economic and social development." In establishing the commission, the UN General Assembly explicitly called attention to two important ideas:

> The well-being of the environment, of economies and of people is inextricably linked.

> Sustainable development involves co-operation on a global scale.

Sustainable development is about integration: developing in a way that benefits the widest possible range of sectors, across borders and even between generations. In other words, our decisions should take into consideration potential impact on society, the environment and the economy, while keeping in mind that: our actions will have impacts elsewhere and our actions will have an impact on the future.

We tend to arrange things compartmentally, by divisions and departments, governments and communities; even households are rarely set up as holistic systems. Ministries of agriculture, finance, the interior and foreign affairs handle the issues that come under their domain. We divide up the tasks of our daily lives: work, rest, errands and holidays. It is not that we *can't* see business, government or home life as a "whole" – making a household budget or a corporate strategy are examples of just this type of exercise – but in the bustle of our complex lives it can be difficult to take the time to see beyond the most immediate or obvious concerns. Often, as the old saying goes, we can't see the forest for the trees.

The concept of sustainable development has been used to articulate several essential shifts of perspective in how we relate to the world around us and, consequently, how we expect governments to make policies that support that world view.

> **"Governments face the complex challenge of finding the right balance between the competing demands on natural and social resources, without sacrificing economic progress."**
> *Sustainable Development: Critical Issues*

First, there is the realisation that economic growth alone is not enough: the economic, social and environmental aspects of any action are *interconnected*. Considering only one of these at a time leads to errors in judgment and "unsustainable" outcomes. Focusing only on profit margins, for example, has historically led to social and environmental damages that cost society in the long run. By the same token, taking care of the environment and providing the services that people need depends at least in part on economic resources.

Will I know it when I see it?

In the first years of the 21st century the term sustainable development has entered the public sphere. No longer restricted to academic and policy debates, the concept has made its way into everyday language and into community activities the world over. When we say the words "sustainable development", what exactly do we mean?

Sustainable development can be:
• spreading the benefits of economic growth to all citizens;

• turning brownfields into ecologically sound urban housing projects;
• increasing educational opportunities for both girls and boys;
• innovating industrial processes to be more energy-efficient and less polluting;
• including citizens and stakeholders in policy-making processes.

Next, the interconnected, or interdependent, nature of sustainable development also calls for going beyond borders – whether they be geographical or institutional – in order to co-ordinate strategies and make good decisions. Problems are rarely easily contained within predefined jurisdictions such as one government agency or a single neighbourhood, and intelligent solutions require co-operation as part of the decision-making process.

Take genetically modified crops, for example. Making decisions on the production, consumption and development of GMOs requires the participation of agriculture, environment, trade, health and research ministries. It requires that these ministries compare evidence and agree on a position within national government so that they can enact workable policies – policies that have the greatest benefit for the least cost. But the need for co-ordination doesn't stop at the national level. Apart from anything else, seeds from genetically modified plants can cross borders, carried by wind or birds, adding an international dimension to the issue. Differing policies between import and export countries leads to confusion and inefficiency in trade, as processed foods containing just one genetically modified ingredient require special labelling and are even banned by some countries.

Finally, thinking about human actions has had to undergo a temporal shift: put simply, we should consider the impact of a given choice beyond the short term. If poorly-managed logging leads to the depletion of a forest in the interest of immediate profit, then the overall result is actually a substantial loss: loss of income over the long term, loss of biodiversity, loss of capacity to absorb carbon dioxide, among other things.

An "honest" approach to timelines is also essential to questions of intergenerational equity: the idea that resources, whether economic, environmental or social, should be utilised and distributed fairly across generations. No single generation should bear an undue burden. This is not only a problem of leaving a clean, healthy planet for future generations, but also concerns pressing problems like meeting the medical, financial and social needs of an ageing population.

The three pillars of sustainable development

At the core of sustainable development is the need to consider "three pillars" *together*: society, the economy and the environment. No matter the context, the basic idea remains the same – people, habitats and economic systems are inter-related. We may be able to ignore that interdependence for a few years or decades, but history has shown that before long we are reminded of it by some type of alarm or crisis.

The fact of the matter is that we depend on ecosystems and the services they provide in order to do what we do: run businesses, build communities, feed our populations and much more. Whether we consider the more obvious, immediately vital examples – the need for soil that can grow food or for clean water to drink – or the less obvious but equally significant things like oxygen production during photosynthesis or waste processing by bacterial decomposers, we cannot avoid the conclusion that we depend on the environment for our existence. If we damage or destroy the capacity of the environment to provide these services we may face consequences for which we are completely unprepared.

> **"As a group, women – and their potential contributions to economic advances, social progress and environmental protection – have been marginalised."**
>
> *Gender and Sustainable Development*

In the same way, the long-term stability and success of societies rely on a healthy and productive population. A society (or communities within a larger society) that faces unrest, poverty and disease will not develop in the long term: social well-being and economic well-being feed off each other, and the whole game depends on a healthy biosphere in which to exist.

Understanding the complex connections and interdependence of the three pillars requires some effort, and the effort has to be constant. Whether we're talking about the duration of political cycles or the length of time the media focuses on a particular issue, the question of our collective attention span is an important one for sustainable development.

The Rio Earth Summit and Agenda 21

In June, 1992, in Rio de Janeiro, representatives from 179 countries came together for the United Nations Conference on Environment and Development, popularly known as the *Rio Earth Summit*. One of the major agreements signed during this meeting was a programme of action called Agenda 21. The 900-page document describes first steps towards initiating Sustainable Development across local, national and international levels as the world moved into the 21st century. Signatories promised to pursue action in four domains:
• Social and Economic Dimension, such as combating poverty and promoting sustainable urban planning;
• Conservation and Management of Resources, such as safeguarding the oceans' fisheries and combating deforestation;

• Strengthening the Role of Major Groups, such as women, local governments and NGO's; and
• Means of Implementation, such as transfer of environmentally-sound technology.

For example, Chapter 28, *Local authorities' initiatives in support of Agenda 21*, calls for the participation of local and regional governments and civil society in the development of Local Agenda 21. Co-ordination in the sustainable development effort from the international level down to local municipalities will ideally make every action more effective. Cities across the world – from Surabaya, Indonesia to Seattle, United States – have implemented such a plan to promote sustainable development at the local level.

Trade-offs

With tens of millions of inhabitants concentrated in a limited space, today's mega-cities struggle to balance the needs of the population with the capacity of the existing infrastructures. Juggling the complex web of activities in urban environments is an ideal place to start thinking through the trade-offs that sustainable development can imply. For instance, everybody might agree that traffic is a nightmare, but making changes to improve the situation inevitably affects many people in a variety of ways, not all positive. Should the city discourage car travel but risk overloading public transport? Should it introduce measures to make traffic move more quickly and risk attracting more vehicles onto the roads? Calculating the financial costs of transport policies is relatively straightforward, but predicting the personal choices and behaviours of those using the urban space is much less so. What will city dwellers and commuters actually decide to do? For example, if the bus service improves, will it attract car drivers or people who might otherwise have walked?

The lesson here is not that it's impossible to improve things, but that improvement means thinking through the links among a number of factors. Less traffic equals shorter travel times and easier movement. Better air quality means a healthier population. The trade-offs, such as taxes or tolls, in exchange for overall improvement of the urban space are being tested in London, Singapore and other cities. The debate as to the success or failure of such schemes shows in a concrete fashion what's at stake. The environmental impacts may seem clear, but what about social equity – the rich can afford to pay a congestion charge that poorer people can't – or the economic impact on shops and other businesses?

On a personal level, the choices may not be so clear-cut either. Imagine you want to avoid supporting the use of pesticides so you choose to buy only organic produce. However, the only organic grocery store in your city is too far to walk or cycle to. Fossil fuels have to be burned to get you there and back. Likewise, you may want to support local producers and avoid the damage air transport causes. But flying flowers to the UK from Africa for instance may cause less harm than importing flowers from nearby Holland that needed heated greenhouses and intensive fertilizer use. And horticulture may benefit more people in Africa than in the Netherlands. In a perfect world, making good choices would be an easier, more coherent task; in the meantime, the concept of sustainable development is helpful for balancing out the vast number of variables and optimising our decisions.

Sustainable development: process or end result?

So, is sustainable development a kind of guiding principle, as many of its supporters would argue? Or rather a concrete goal or set of goals that can be measured, evaluated and deemed "achieved"? Looking at the massive body of literature on the subject reveals plenty of support for both these points of view and several other possibilities. Really, though, there is no obligation to choose among these options. Whether we are talking about the abolition of slavery, universal education, democracy or any of the "sea changes" that previous generations have undergone, we are always in a constant process of translating big ideas into concrete practices. And this always involves multiple experiments, learning, failures, mistakes and a constant effort at adapting and refining our methods.

Sustainable development is also a means for considering the relationships of things to each other in order to propose viable solutions. As the Brundtland report puts it, "sustainable development is not a fixed state of harmony but rather a process of change..." It is a way of forcing ourselves to look at factors we might rather ignore in favour of short-term benefit, as in the case of a polluting industry that worries primarily about this year's profits, or a pension plan that doesn't account for the increase in the number of retirees relative to the number of subscribers.

Brice Lalonde, former Minister of the Environment in France, offers the following definition: *"To me, it refers to how the economy should enable us to live better lives while improving our environment and our societies, from now on and within a globalised world."* In this view, sustainable development frames the possibilities for progress: the economy is a vehicle that helps us reach the overall, collective, goal of improving quality of life *globally.* Success comes through putting all three pillars on the same progressive trajectory, or path.

It might be useful, then, to see the advent of sustainable development as a significant change in how people and governments perceive their activities, their roles and responsibilities: from primary emphasis on increasing material wealth to a more complex, interconnected model of the human development process.

Sustainable development is therefore:

> a conceptual framework: a way of changing the predominant world view to one that is more holistic and balanced;

> a process: a way of applying the principles of integration – across space and time – to all decisions; and

> an end goal: identifying and fixing the specific problems of resource depletion, health care, social exclusion, poverty, unemployment, etc.

Easier said than done?

Society, the environment and the economy – doesn't that cover just about everything? One of the first things we notice when trying to understand sustainable development is the vastness of the topic. Taking into account the economic, social and environmental

Low-tech high-impact: insecticide-treated mosquito nets

Sustainable development means using all the tools at our disposal to promote well-being. As the following example shows, technologies don't have to be high-tech to achieve significant change.

Malaria kills a child every 30 seconds and over a million people every year. Apart from children its main victims are pregnant women. Most of those who die are in Africa. Poor people and communities with limited access to health care are the worst affected.

Malaria is responsible for a "growth penalty" of 1.3% a year in some countries and contributes to the substantial differences in GDP between countries with and without the disease. It can affect the tourist industry since travellers prefer to avoid badly affected areas. Traders' unwillingness to travel to and invest in malaria areas can leave markets underdeveloped. Farmers cannot take the risk of planting labour-intensive crops because of malaria's impact on labour during the harvest season.

In some countries, malaria may account for as much as 40% of public health expenditure, 30 to 50% of inpatient admissions and up to 60% of outpatient visits. It stops children from going to school and can cause permanent neurological damage. It hits the earnings of sick workers and can ruin families who have to pay for drugs, other health care and transport to hospital.

The parasite that causes the disease is becoming more resistant to antimalarial drugs, and no new treatments are expected soon. Likewise, the mosquitoes that transmit the disease are becoming more resistant to insecticides.

A simple technology to prevent deaths and the spread of the disease exists: insecticide treated mosquito nets. The nets generate a chemical halo that extends beyond the fabric itself to repel or deter mosquitoes from biting or shortens the mosquito's life span so it can't transmit malaria.

They also reduce the quantity of insecticide that needs to be sprayed in homes and elsewhere. But while the technology is simple, using it effectively depends on getting a number of things right:

- People need to be convinced of the utility of the nets and shown how to use them through education and social marketing campaigns.
- Taxes and tariffs on mosquito nets, netting materials and insecticides should be waived.
- Encouraging local manufacturers and suppliers can help reduce costs so that nets are affordable.
- Nets that can last for years without having to be retreated with insecticide need to become widespread.

In Kenya, from 2004 to 2006, the number of young children sleeping under insecticide-treated nets increased tenfold thanks to a programme of free mass distribution. There were 44% fewer deaths than among children not protected by nets. Kenya's success suggests three ingredients which all need to be present for malaria control to succeed: high political commitment from the government, strong technical assistance from the WHO and adequate funding from international donors.

To find out more, visit the website of the Roll Back Malaria Partnership launched in 1998 by the WHO, UNICEF, the United Nations Development Programme and the World Bank: *www.rollbackmalaria.org.*

aspects of development can ultimately include a wide variety of concepts, policies and projects. So wide, some would say, that it loses its usefulness as a concept.

This could in part explain why, in spite of its popularity and rapid acceptance by some members of government, civil society, countless companies and many cities, the concept of sustainable development has not yet translated into widespread changes in either behaviours or policy, and this after more than a decade of efforts. Early supporters of the concept had hoped for rapid progress, but the complexity of the problems at hand, their

---

Women and Sustainable Development

"At present, the female half of the world's human capital is undervalued and underutilised the world over... Better use of the world's female population could increase economic growth, reduce poverty, enhance societal well-being, and help ensure sustainable development in all countries."

Gender and Sustainable Development: Maximising the Economic, Social and Environmental Role of Women

When it comes to improving economies, societies and preserving the environment, women have a central role. Across the globe, per capita income is lowest in countries where women are significantly less educated than men, suggesting that investing in women is a first step to raising everyone's well-being. In Africa, studies show that giving women equal access to capital could increase crop yields by up to 20%. But developed countries would benefit from fuller use of women's potential too, for instance the UK's GDP could rise by 2% by better harnessing women's skills. Improving education for girls and women also has social benefits, including lower fertility rates, reduced infant and mother mortality, and improved nutrition for all members of the family. Data from developing countries indicate that one to three years of maternal schooling reduces child mortality by 15% while an equivalent level of paternal schooling achieves only a 6% reduction.

Women are also on the environmental "frontlines". Wangari Maathai won the 2004 Nobel Peace Prize for her work with the Green Belt Project, reforesting vast areas of Kenya. The 30 million trees women have planted through the Project provide firewood and shelter, and improve local climate and soil. As Maathai said in her acceptance speech, "throughout Africa, women are the primary caretakers, holding significant responsibility for tilling the land and feeding their families. As a result, they are often the first to become aware of environmental damage as resources become scarce and incapable of sustaining their families." As Maathi proves, women often hold the solutions, too.

Clearly, improving the situation of women worldwide is a critical first step for sustainable development – indeed this was one of the conclusions of Agenda 21.

---

reach across cities, regions and beyond national borders, and the difficulties inherent in changing people's perceptions and actions have all contributed to frustrating those hopes.

Adding this level of complexity to decision-making processes most probably necessitates changes in previous patterns of behaviour – whether at the level of individual consumption or international law. And change is almost never easy, even when it is obviously necessary. It is particularly difficult when it might involve real or perceived sacrifices on the part of one "pillar", industry, country or generation in favour of another.

It is still quite common to hear that sustainable development is primarily about the environment. And while it is true that the concept grew out of thinking about the dangers of environmentally unsustainable practices such as the damage done to ozone layer by CFCs or the damage to soils and water supplies due to pesticides, sustainable development has also always included the social dimension.

In any case, to get caught up in an argument over whether sustainable development is more about the environment or about people is to miss the point: it is the connection of humans, their economies and societies to the ecosystems that support them which defines sustainable development. "Environmental problems are really social problems anyway," said Sir Edmund Hilary, the first man to conquer Mount Everest. "They begin with people as the cause and end with people as the victims."

So really we can see sustainable development as a big theory, a process, or as practical guidelines for making solid development decisions that do not blindly seek growth in one area only to cause damage in another. We can choose to support any or all of these positions, provided that we have the information we need to make honest assessments about our activities and their impact – and make some of the "tough" decisions that good management often requires.

Applying the principles of sustainable development is really nothing more than applying the principles of sound management to all our resources, like we would if we wanted to create a prosperous business or build a new house. Rather than overlook potential conflicts, we can plan ahead, integrating considerations of what counts from the beginning. Of course this is easier said than done:

spending money now to prevent something that "might" happen in the future is a challenge for us. Just as spending money to fix a bad situation "elsewhere" is also tough. Really, though, the future is right around the corner, and in our globalised world what seems far can become very suddenly close. By following the example of the ever-increasing number of individuals, businesses and governments who make planning decisions within a sustainable development framework, we ensure ourselves and our children a brighter future.

Find Out More

... FROM OECD

On the Internet

For a general introduction to OECD work on sustainable development, visit *www.oecd.org/sustainabledevelopment.*

Publications

Sustainable Development: Critical Issues (2001):
Following a mandate from OECD Ministers in 1998, this report stresses the urgency to address some of the most pressing challenges for sustainable development. It reviews the conceptual foundations of sustainable development, its measurement, and the institutional reforms needed to make it operational. It then discusses how international trade and investment, as well as development co-operation, can contribute to sustainable development on a global basis, and reviews the experience of OECD countries in using market-based, regulatory and technology policies to reach sustainability goals in a cost-effective way.

Also of interest

OECD Contribution to the United Nations Commission on Sustainable Development 15: Energy for Sustainable Development (2007):
Under the theme of "Energy for Sustainable Development", this brochure presents policy findings from OECD, IEA and NEA reports relating to energy, climate change and sustainable development.
It focuses on four main topics:
I) widening energy access in developing countries,
II) increasing energy research and development and dissemination,
III) promoting energy efficiency and diversity, and IV) benefiting from energy-related climate change policies.

Gender and Sustainable Development: Maximising the Economic, Social and Environmental Role of Women (2008):
As a group, women – and their potential contributions to economic advances, social progress and environmental protection – have been marginalised. Better use of the world's female population could increase economic growth, reduce poverty, enhance societal well-being, and help ensure sustainable development in all countries. Closing the gender gap depends on enlightened government policies which take gender dimensions into account.

This report is a contribution by the OECD to the UNCSD and its cross-cutting work on gender. It aims to increase understanding of the role of women in maintaining the three pillars – economic, social and environmental – of sustainable development.

Advancing Sustainable Development, an *OECD Policy Brief* (2006):
This Policy Brief looks at progress towards sustainable development in the OECD and its member countries, and at what more can be done to advance sustainable development in the Organisation's work and policy discussions.

All titles are available at *www.oecd.org/sustainabledevelopment.*

... AND OTHER SOURCES

Our Common Future ("The Brundtland Report")
(*www.un-documents.net/wced-ocf.htm*):
This 1987 report from the United Nations World Commission on Environment and Development placed environmental concerns on the political agenda and laid the foundation for the 1992 Earth Summit and the adoption of Agenda 21, the Rio Declaration and the Commission on Sustainable Development.

3

In today's interdependent world, economic trends that start in one country affect many others, and national economies are affected by the internationalisation of production and international trade. Resource management, pollution control and climate phenomena are all issues that by their nature reach beyond geographic borders, making the challenges of sustainability a priority shared by countries and communities everywhere.

Challenges of
a Global World

By way of introduction...

Life in Ahoto in the state of Jigawa, Nigeria has followed the same rhythm for centuries. In this village of thatched mud huts, farmers eke out a subsistence income from the difficult lands to the south of the Sahara desert. But things have begun to change recently: solar power has come to Ahoto and brought with it substantial improvements people's lives.

Garba Bello, head of the village, is very happy about these changes. As a recipient of one of the household lighting systems (costing about four dollars per month), he enjoys what solar lighting has done for his household, and most of all for his village. "The difference is great," he says. "People now go out at night and chat. Before, you could not even see your neighbour's house in the night."

The solar power project has brought more than just light to Ahoto and the two other villages participating in the region. A new shopping area is driving business development and creating much needed economic activity. Educational opportunities are also on the rise: women now attend classes at night and children can do their homework.

A collaborative effort by NGOs, the state government and foreign aid, the Jigawa State project takes a promising use of alternative energy a step further than previous projects that focused on only one use, such as pumping water. By attempting to address *all* of a village's energy needs, from education and commerce to security and women's advancement – the project gives participants the means to move forward simultaneously in all areas of their development.

The benefits extend beyond the social and economic to questions of health. Villagers now have access to clean water from more efficient solar pumps that draw water from deeper non-polluted sources and distribute it to household and communal taps. Easier access to relatively low-cost potable water also frees up considerable amounts of time that used to go to collecting water by bucket or hand pumping from wells. Activities that had to end at sunset can now continue, and in healthier circumstances. Dangerous and dirty kerosene lamps are now rarely lit. This has significant implications for health. About 1.5 million people die prematurely each year from the effects of indoor pollution from burning wood, charcoal and waste, more than from malaria, almost as many as from tuberculosis and almost half as many as from HIV/AIDS.

It is a solution that is elegant in its simplicity – bypassing, or "leapfrogging", traditional technology to move directly to one that is cleaner and far more sustainable. Yet projects like Ahoto's are still too few compared to the vast energy needs of the developing world, where, on present trends 1.4 billion will still be without access to mains electricity in 2030.

In Chapters 1 and 2, we saw how massive growth can create as many problems as it solves, some of them serious and potentially very destructive. Equally significant is the fact that growth may benefit some groups and leave others behind, a fact that is masked by indicators such as rates of increase in a country's GDP. And finally, if a short-term increase in wealth comes at the expense of long-term well-being and or survival, then it is not really "good" growth in any meaningful sense.

▶ In this chapter we turn to sustainable development to formulate the central question that ties together our contemporary globalised society: how can we grow in a way that maintains the achievements in health and living standards in the developed world and continues to raise living standards for those who still lag behind without permanently damaging the world we depend on? Can we see more development in the style that has benefited Ahoto in recent years?

Going global: an old process on a new scale

The phenomenon of globalisation has received a considerable amount of attention in recent years as social scientists, political pundits and cultural critics have tried to explain how it has transformed our world. Is it really new, though? For as long as explorers have had the means to cover great distances, people have sought to know, understand and profit from what lay beyond the familiarity of their own communities.

The great periods of exploration and colonisation attest to this desire, one that combines many different motivations. To learn about the world, to seek out better means of survival when local methods had failed, to seek fame and fortune, to trade for what one lacked, to bring glory to the state – these various driving forces interacted and pushed human societies forward to a world that became more and more connected over time.

Nowadays, globalisation is not about a few rich countries trading with far-off lands. Geopolitics, technology and finance have transformed consumption and production patterns across the globe. Over the past decade alone, around a billion workers have joined the global marketplace. Better communication tools and falling transport costs have expanded the range of goods and services in national markets. The combination of a greater supply of cheap labour alongside technologies that facilitate trade means that "value chains" – the numerous steps involved in transforming materials, knowledge and labour into saleable products – are spread across the globe. What is new about the globalisation of the last 30 years or so is that we are nearing a point where connection is not the *exception* but the *rule*.

According to the World Trade Organization, international trade has consistently increased with yearly growth rates of around 6% over the last decade. China is a leader here, with merchandising

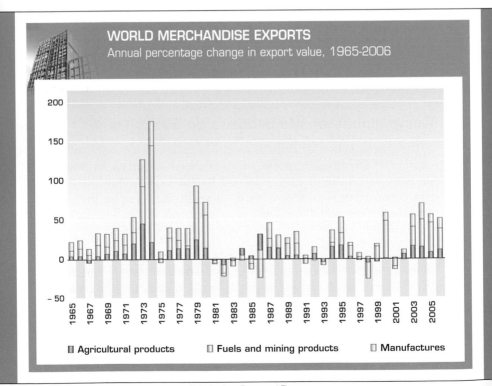

WORLD MERCHANDISE EXPORTS
Annual percentage change in export value, 1965-2006

☐ Agricultural products　　☐ Fuels and mining products　　☐ Manufactures

Source: UNCTAD (2008), *Development and Globalization: Facts and Figures.*

export increases of 27%, while developing countries' share of world merchandise exports reached an all time record of 36%. It is a fact that our economies are now dependent on international exchanges for their continued progress.

Whether we are talking about trade and investment, politics or culture, examples of linkages and interdependence surround us. We need only think of the food on our plates, the clothes on our backs or a website like YouTube: the sources of what fills our daily lives are multiple and geographically diverse. We sample the world's offerings every day, rarely realising how all of those connections have come to be, or how they interact.

These changes in our daily lives are related to international developments with a substantially increased movement of money and things: trade rules have been "liberalised" or modified to encourage international competition; corporations have expanded beyond their country of origin to new markets around the globe. All this moving and mixing has opened up possibilities for exchange, commercial expansion and overall growth, making the world, on average, a richer place.

> **"Recent years have indeed witnessed striking changes in the global economic landscape, confirming the role of trade as a driving force in economic development and providing an indication of the potential for further trade liberalisation, under the right conditions, to benefit the global economy broadly."**
>
> Douglas Lippoldt, *Trading Up: Economic Perspectives on Development Issues in the Multilateral Trading System*

This "new" global dimension – economic, political and social – offers seemingly endless opportunities. But these opportunities are not equally available to all, and means to restore the balance have to be found. Nobel Prize economist Joseph Stiglitz has written recently about one of these, the fact that economic globalisation has left politics trying to play catch up. He points out that globalisation has in some ways changed the role of the nation-state since so many important issues now reach beyond the country level. In spite of this shift, Stiglitz notes, "there has yet to be created at the international level the kinds of democratic global institutions that can deal effectively with the problems globalization has created."

A two-tier world

Globalisation has increased our ties across geographical boundaries and perhaps transformed the way we think of «the world». Yet for all our increased connections, we obviously don't share the same circumstances, lifestyles or opportunities. As long as we have lived in large communities, the "haves" and the "have nots" have existed side by side. In today's media-rich culture, it is hard not to be aware of the glaring disparities in living standards in different parts of the world, even as we all participate in the same global economy.

Where we are born, grow up and live makes a big difference. An average child growing up today in Europe has vaccinations, dental care and educational opportunities, not to mention a more than adequate diet. He or she can look forward to higher education, travel, employment and retirement provided, at least in part, by a stable government. Economic growth in such OECD countries hovers around 2.5%, enough to maintain and hopefully continue improving quality of life provided that resources are managed wisely.

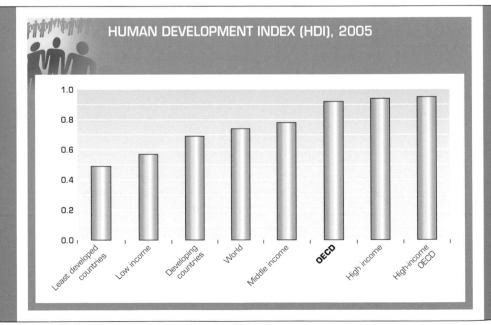

HUMAN DEVELOPMENT INDEX (HDI), 2005

Source: UNDP (2007), *Human Development Report 2007/2008.*

> "Despite progress, huge challenges remain. Gross inequality is still prevalent in the world and global problems – such as climate change – continue to grow."
>
> Richard Manning, *Development Co-operation Report 2007*

Some other countries have, after long periods of no or slow growth, recently gained speed – at least in terms of increases in their Gross Domestic Product (GDP). Still, many of their citizens are living "in another world". In India, where growth has averaged 8.5% for the last 4 years, 300 million people still live on less than the equivalent of a dollar per day. Africa has shown encouraging growth too – averaging above 5% per year for the continent as a whole in 2007, the fourth successive year of record growth – yet life expectancy in many African countries remains shockingly low. In Swaziland, people live on average 39.6 years – less than half the average lifespan in Japan, the country with the highest average.

Indeed, the different speeds at which countries are meeting basic development goals leaves us asking: Will economic growth translate into equal opportunities for citizens in the near future? What else can be done to make sure that more of the world's underdeveloped communities gain ground in as fast and efficient a way as possible?

North and South, High and Low

For a long time, when speaking about the differences in wealth and equality, we have used common shorthand references such as "developed and developing countries" or "North and South", the latter having grown out of a geographical reference, comparing the US and Canada with Latin and South America; Europe with Africa.

Today its meaning has evolved into an economic one, referring to the differences between high income countries and poorer countries that are behind in various areas of development: income, education levels and access to health care, among others. With rapidly growing economies like India, China, Brazil and Russia that do not easily fit into either category, the picture is less and less clear. What is evident is that some countries (the "North") are able to provide an advanced level of social services, income and environmental quality to their citizens, a level that by almost all statistical measures improves year by year, while many others (the "South") have not reached the basic level.

For some commentators, this sort of division is the natural order of things. But for more and more of today's citizens this two-tiered system is not only unfair, it will also be detrimental in the long term, even to those of us living in the top tier.

National growth has global consequences

For China, India and the other emerging economies, growth is happening rapidly, bringing with it both the positive and negative consequences of intensified production and increased economic activity. Because of their sheer size, the choices these countries make as to how to direct their growth have a huge impact worldwide. Media everywhere noted with gravity a symbolic passage in 2007: China is now the world's largest producer of CO_2 emissions. But we cannot forget that its emissions per capita are still a fraction of those of OECD countries. The principle of "shared but differentiated responsibility" between developed and developing countries tries to take this into account. Outlined at the 2002 Johannesburg Summit on Sustainable Development, the principle recognises historical differences in the contributions of developed and developing states to global environmental problems, and differences in their respective economic and technical capacity to tackle these problems.

> **"The global importance of rapidly emerging economies is growing as they become major economic and trade partners, competitors, resource users and polluters on a level that compares to the largest of OECD countries."**
> *OECD Environmental Outlook to 2030*

Environmental consequences such as climate change respect no borders, driving home the necessity for a global perspective on pollution. To reach their current sizes of about $14 trillion and $16 trillion annual GDP respectively, the United States and European economies drew heavily on natural resources and depended almost entirely on fossil fuels. Today's changing climate is largely due to the rich countries' historical emissions. The economic model that drove this development had serious consequences for the environment, such as the permanent destruction of species and ecosystems and an increase in atmospheric carbon dioxide that most scientists believe is already changing our climate. Now the model, and its consequences, are being replicated by other countries at an accelerated pace.

The global nature of our economy means that we are increasingly linked to other countries. Disruptions half-way across the world come home in a dramatic way when they drive up the price of food or petrol at home, or result in a deployment of armed forces.

People living in regions where economic prospects are dim may choose, by whatever means possible, to emigrate to wealthier destinations. While the positive impacts of immigration in OECD countries are well-established – providing much-needed labour for example – humanitarian and economic emigration can put a burden on countries' social systems of both the country people leave and the one they go to, especially in situations of crisis and when the "host" country is a developing country.

By 2030, the world population is expected to reach 8.2 billion people from 6.5 billion today. Such projections from the most recent OECD Environmental Outlook can seem like daunting increases when we consider that the world's resources are already stretched to capacity in many respects. Where will that growth take place? A large part of it will be in the fast-developing economies of Brazil, Russia, India, Indonesia, China and South Africa – known as the BRIICS. What form will that growth take? How can we all shift to more sustainable models of growth?

A level playing field

Those who criticise the environmental record of rapidly developing countries run into an interesting debate regarding the "right" of developing countries to pollute or to have access to more advanced, less damaging technologies. Europe and the United States spent several hundred years practicing rampant deforestation and industrial pollution before putting in place tight regulation. Why should China and Indonesia have to play the game by different rules from those followed by developed countries in the past?

> **"There can be no moral grounds for expecting China and India selectively to curb their economic growth simply because world energy demand is rising unacceptably, with associated risks of supply interruptions, high prices and damage to the environment. These are global problems to be tackled on a global basis."**
> *World Energy Outlook 2007: China and India Insights*

Indeed it is often perceived as unfair for rich countries to lecture poor countries on resource use when the developed world is responsible, by its size, history and volume of activity, for the majority of resource consumption and the problems that ensue from irresponsible development. While all major emitters must act, the developed countries need to take the lead in addressing climate change. With global issues such as ozone depletion, climate change and biodiversity loss, everyone feels the effects of development when it is unsustainable; everyone should also feel the benefits when it is sustainable. Whether we are talking about people's quality of life or sound natural resource management, success depends on the participation of countries, regions and localities at all stages of development.

So then the question becomes one of *how* to fairly share the burdens of achieving well-managed growth. Developing countries have to cope with climate change and other problems they did not create, and do not have the same means as developed countries in tackling them. The developed countries can help by providing technologies, finance and know-how to tackle these issues, over and above regular development assistance.

The international community has engaged in various forms of development aid for over half a century; billions of dollars have been spent on different types of projects designed to spur growth and improve living standards in the poorer countries. The current international consensus is that each OECD country spends 0.7% of gross national income (GNI) on foreign aid versus 0.3% at present in order to reach global development targets such as the Millennium Development Goals. Aid to Africa alone is expected to reach $51 billion by 2010 from $40 billion in 2006. But making sure that aid is directed to sustainable projects adds another layer of complication.

Closing the development gap sustainably

Meeting the needs of today without diminishing the capacity of future generations to meet their needs: sometimes discussions on sustainable development have tended to focus more on the second half of this of this phrase – the effect of our actions on the future – than on the first half. Yet meeting the needs of today is anything but obvious, easy or conflict-free. If sustainable development is to do this, then tackling the "development gap" – the vast difference in income, access to health care, sanitation and education that exists between the wealthier and poorer countries – must figure among its most pressing projects.

> **"Addressing the challenges of the globalizing economy means addressing the needs of those people and countries that remain on the fringes, as well as those which are emerging into the mainstream."**
> Robert Zoellick, World Bank President, OECD/World Bank Conference on Sustainable and Inclusive Development: Going for Growth

"It is not easy for men to rise whose qualities are thwarted by poverty," observed the 1st century Roman poet Juvenal. The question of what causes poverty and what can reduce or eradicate it has long been a source of much debate, one of the fundamental questions facing the human community. We all have some idea or image in our heads of what constitutes poverty. It's not just a question of possessions – poor people in rich countries own more things than most people elsewhere. Research on the topic points to a more complex combination of the material, social and political aspects of poverty, where lack of access to information, political participation, health care and education among other things contributes to blocking the dynamic that would make lasting development possible. Being ill, hungry, or having to flee violence forces people to redirect their energy to the act of survival, without the luxury of long-term considerations. Addressing the basic needs of the world's poorest people would go a long way in fostering development in today's global economy, but it would obviously require a global approach.

Early promoters of sustainable development realised that to make the substantial changes required to produce meaningful results would require a global effort. No person, municipality, region or even country could alone transform the ideas and practices driving development. The increasingly important role of international agreements on the common concerns of the global community – trade, multinationals, poverty reduction to name only a few – attest to the need for international arena to solve problems of global significance.

The UN, OECD and other international organisations are struggling to bring sustainable development to the forefront. Other organisations including the World Bank, International Monetary Fund and World Trade Organisation are seeking means to incorporate sustainability as a basic principle in their economic operations. These institutions have brought national governments with a diverse range of views and means together to the same table to hash out their differences in the interest of improving development practices. At the same time, local and regional governments are joining forces to compare

The Millennium Development Goals

Officially established in 2000 at the UN Millennium Summit, the Millennium Development Goals identify 8 development goals and under these 18 concrete targets to be reached by 2015. Agreed by 192 UN Member states, they represent a global agreement to achieve results in the most critical areas of human progress.

1. Eradicate extreme poverty and hunger

Reduce by half the proportion of people living on less than a dollar a day.

Reduce by half the proportion of people who suffer from hunger.

2. Achieve universal primary education

Ensure that all boys and girls complete a full course of primary schooling.

3. Promote gender equality and empower women

Eliminate gender disparity in primary and secondary education preferably by 2005, and in all levels by 2015.

4. Reduce child mortality

Reduce by two-thirds the mortality rate among children under five.

5. Improve maternal health

Reduce, by three-quarters the maternal mortality ratio.

6. Combat HIV/AIDS, malaria and other diseases

Halt and begin to reverse the spread of HIV/AIDS.

Halt and begin to reverse the incidence of malaria and other major diseases.

7. Ensure environmental sustainability

Integrate the principles of sustainable development into country policies and programmes; reverse loss of environmental resources.

Reduce by half the proportion of people without sustainable access to safe drinking water.

Achieve significant improvement in lives of at least 100 million slum dwellers, by 2020.

8. Develop a global partnership for development

Develop further an open, rule-based, predictable, non-discriminatory trading and financial system.

Address the least developed countries' special needs.

Address the special needs of landlocked countries and small island developing states.

Deal comprehensively with developing countries' debt problems.

In cooperation with the developing countries, develop decent and productive work for youth.

In cooperation with pharmaceutical companies, provide access to affordable essential drugs in developing countries.

In cooperation with the private sector, make available the benefits of new technologies – especially information and communications technologies.

The MDG Monitor tracks the progress towards achieving these goals. It gives an overview of the principle targets that come under each goal, indicators for measuring progress and examples of success stories.

www.mdgmonitor.org/goal1.cfm

their experiences and work together, often across great geographical distance. All in all, governments are starting to realise that they need to undertake a more collaborative, open approach to problems that are more crosscutting.

The idea of being able to improve the lives of the poorest through global action has taken hold over the course of this century, culminating with the Millennium Development Goals – an effort to attack the problem in a co-ordinated way and on a global scale. Originating in the OECD guidelines for development, the MDGs, as they are known, represent a concerted effort on the part of the world community to address the persistent problems of underdevelopment.

Tools for sustainable growth

With the exception of a few rapidly growing economies, growth in the developing countries has on the whole been inconsistent and insufficient to bridge the huge differences in living standards within these countries and compared to the developed countries. Recent indicators show that Sub-Saharan Africa has begun to see the rates of growth comparable to the rest of the world, albeit from a low starting point, but this has not yet translated into great gains in a number of critical areas. For example, the number of people in Sub-Saharan Africa with access to drinking water increased by 10 million per year over 1990-2004. However, population sizes have grown even faster, so the number of people without access has increased by about 60 million.

Each country's historical, economic, social and political context is unique, but the basic principles of sustainable development apply to all. Economic growth is essential, but growth alone, without understanding all the factors that contribute to well-being including social, environmental, institutional and cultural considerations, does not produce sustainable poverty reduction. While it is true that economic growth generally correlates with overall improvements in quality of life, higher levels of education and life expectancy at the country level, this does not tell us:

➤ how this growth is achieved

➤ whether or not it is lasting

➤ who benefits and who might be left behind.

Countries with highly valued natural resources such as diamonds, metals or oil have the means to increase overall economic development by selling these resources on world markets. Still, this may result in no improvement in people's lives if this income remains in the hands of very few and is not used in any way that benefits the population. If these resources are non-renewable, or poorly-managed, then the income they produce will at some point cease to be a source of growth – unless profits from them are reinvested in other projects or funds that are sustainable over time. Finally, activities that are profitable today may be degrading the environment for tomorrow. In sum, short-term growth may mean nothing in terms of long-term stability, and it can produce net environmental and social loss if the stocks and the capital generated from them are not managed *sustainably*.

Pro-poor growth

So the question is how to create growth that allows the poor to achieve real, lasting advances. Economists and development theorists call this *pro-poor growth*. According to this way of thinking, it is not enough to achieve average growth rates of a certain percentage. Growth should specifically benefit poor women and men and allow them to reap the benefits of increases in economic activity and income so that they can access a path of consistent improvement in their living conditions.

Aid for Trade

Trade offers real potential to boost growth and meet development goals. Yet developing countries often lack some of the elements necessary to reaping these benefits: such things as reliable banking systems, functioning telecommunications or good roads and ports for transport.
Aid for Trade is development assistance specifically dedicated to helping countries eliminate these barriers and take advantage of trade opportunities.

It includes assistance in:

• negotiating trade agreements

• capacity building (creating the conditions to enable policies and projects to succeed)

• marketing

• meeting international standards for quality

The global trade organisation, WTO, and the OECD work together on assessing the effectiveness of Aid for Trade measures in contributing to international development.

What exactly are the means of meeting development goals? We all know some of the basic elements such as capital, health, education, technology. Approaches to providing aid and fostering growth are diverse. Development specialists describe three major avenues: official development assistance or ODA, foreign direct investment (FDI), and trade. Though these are distinct categories in a definitional sense, they work together in practical terms. For example, ODA funds might be directed to measures intended to attract FDI or develop trade, as in the case of Aid for Trade.

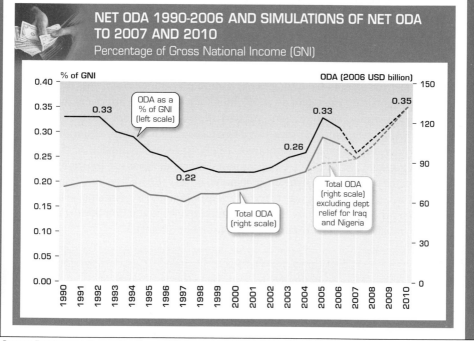

NET ODA 1990-2006 AND SIMULATIONS OF NET ODA TO 2007 AND 2010

Percentage of Gross National Income (GNI)

Source: Development Co-operation Report 2007.   StatLink : http://dx.doi.org/10.1787/470848625256

New forms of aid have also begun to play an important part in helping achieve development targets. Large private foundations such as the Bill and Melinda Gates foundation and public-private partnerships like the Global Fund to fight AIDS, Malaria and Tuberculosis and the Global Alliance for Vaccines and Immunization (GAVI) have had a significant impact on how aid programmes are conceptualised and implemented, even though they represent a relatively small percentage of the funding pie.

Donor countries and agencies have certainly become aware of the importance of sustainability issues and are working to ensure that environmental considerations are integrated into the Poverty Reduction Strategies of recipient countries. The United Nations Environment Programme (UNEP) and the UN Development Programme (UNDP) oversee many of these efforts as part of the Poverty-Environment Initiative. In turn, the OECD's Development Assistance Committee (DAC) keeps track of these projects, in accordance with the Paris Declaration on Aid Effectiveness. The objective is to ensure that environmental concerns are integrated into development strategies, although for the time being progress is uneven.

Another example of the international effort to ensure that environmental considerations are included in development initiatives is Strategic Environmental Assessment (SEA). While Environmental Impact Statements have long been required by donor countries, they often represent a last item on a checklist for a project, an approach that leads to conflict of interest and missed opportunities. Since 2001, both donor and recipient countries have been passing legislation to undertake SEA for development programmes likely to have an impact on the environment. With SEAs, environmental considerations are integrated from the conception of national or regional Poverty Reduction Strategies. But we still have a long way to go before sustainability assessments of all three pillars are routinely conducted and Poverty Reduction Strategies are transformed into Sustainable Development Strategies.

Achieving positive revision to forest policies in Ghana

Issue

An examination of the Ghana Poverty Reduction Strategy (GPRS) identified potential conflicts between the forest policy (aimed at broadening the resource base of the wood industry) and environmental protection of river system bank-side ecosystems. As a result, Ghana's forest policy was modified. In less than six months, the government had set up nurseries to raise bamboo and rattan plants to increase the supply of raw materials for the industry, thereby helping

protect riverbanks from uncontrolled harvesting of wild bamboo and rattan.

Key benefits
- Reduced pressure on primary forests and fragile river ecosystems.
- Creation of new timber resources.
- Employment.

Source: IMF (2006), "Ghana: Poverty Reduction Strategy Paper Annual Progress Report", *IMF Country Report,* No. 06/226, IMF, Washington, D.C.

Making aid count

There is a need to ensure that the development objectives of countries giving aid and those receiving it are co-ordinated and mutually reinforcing. In March 2005, representatives from non-governmental agencies and over 100 countries – both donors and recipients of aid – came together to sign an international agreement in this direction: The Paris Declaration on Aid Effectiveness.

> **"We… resolve to take far-reaching and monitorable actions to reform the ways we deliver and manage aid … we recognise that while the volumes of aid and other development resources must increase to achieve these goals, aid effectiveness must increase significantly as well to support partner country efforts to strengthen governance and improve development performance."**
>
> *Paris Declaration on Aid Effectiveness*

Co-ordinating the efforts of different donor and recipient governments is challenge enough – but add to that all the other actors involved in the development process such as NGOs, the media, or financial institutions, and we soon see why the infusion of capital is simply not sufficient. Donors must be organised and coherent in their approach – what is called "harmonisation." They should base their efforts on the needs expressed by recipient governments' national strategies.

Donors, recipients and professionals working in project implementation realise that without better co-ordination, local engagement and accountability, aid is likely to fall short of its targets. The Paris Declaration on Aid Effectiveness of 2005, an agreement signed by donors and recipient governments as well as multilateral aid organisations, reflects this commitment to a more coherent, realistic approach to meeting development goals.

Realising and articulating the need for better, more focused co-ordination is an important step, but it is only a beginning. Closing the development gap depends on building sustainable, healthy societies – removing the barriers that impede progress and bringing into the discussion such things as human rights, gender equality, peace and security. These more complex and diffuse elements pose a challenge for monitoring, but the need for policy coherence on these items is included in the reviews (know as "peer reviews") the OECD carries out of its member countries' development assistance efforts.

Going forward

In spite of the amount of aid, investment and trade-related growth, the development gap remains. One reason for this is a lack of co-ordination. Sometimes policy aims conflict, as when donor countries provide aid for health systems and at the same time try to attract doctors and nurses from the developing world.

Countries are starting to address what has to happen to make aid, trade, investment and other economic policies perform better in order to achieve lasting development results. In specialist language, this is called "policy coherence for development" which means making sure that the economic objectives of donor countries are coherent and do not undermine each other. For example, subsidies to domestic farmers or fishers do not negate gains in opening world markets, export credits or investment incentives do not conflict with the goals of development assistance policies do not interfere with building human and social capital, and so on.

> "Providing aid to improve a country's ability to engage in agricultural trade while maintaining trade barriers or measures that keep the developing country's goods out renders aid inefficient and hampers growth."
>
> *Agriculture: Improving Policy Coherence for Development*
> (an OECD Policy Brief)

According to a much-quoted saying, "Give a man a fish and you feed him for a day. Teach him how to fish and you feed him for a lifetime." But is this true? What if he overfishes? Or more efficient boats from elsewhere take all the accessible stocks? Or pesticides are washed into the breeding grounds and drive the fish away? Teaching "how to fish" involves much more than knowing how to cast a net. We have to understand the critical nature of linkages – how things relate to each other. And it is here that applying the principles of sustainability throughout the development process takes on its full meaning. The goal is not for the developing world to "catch up" with the bad habits of the industrialised countries, but rather for the developing and developed countries to co-operate in instituting sustainable growth across the board. If we are to put both richer and poorer countries on a path to development that lasts, we all have to start fishing sustainably.

Find Out More

... FROM OECD

On the Internet

For an introduction to OECD work on sustainable development and development in general, visit *www.oecd.org/sustainabledevelopment* and *www.oecd.org/development*.

Publications

Trading up: Economic Perspectives on Development Issues in the Multilateral Trading System (2006):
Trade liberalisation is a hotly debated issue, especially concerning developing countries. This book considers trade and development from an economic perspective to examine these emotive issues using empirical approaches and dispassionate analysis.

Applying Strategic Environmental Assessment (2006):
Strategic Environmental Assessment (SEA) is a tool for integrating the principles of sustainable development into country programmes and policies. This volume explains the key steps for its application based on recent experiences. Twelve points are identified for the practical application of SEA in development co-operation, along with a checklist of questions and hands-on case studies. Evaluation and capacity development for SEA processes are also addressed.

Trade that Benefits the Environment and Development: Opening Markets for Environmental Goods and Services (2005):
This collection of studies is a practical tool to help negotiators navigate the numerous, complex issues in international discussions over liberalising trade in environmental goods and services.

Also of interest

Toward Sustainable Agriculture (2008):
This OECD contribution to the UN Commission on Sustainable Development promotes policy coherence in terms of agricultural subsidy reform and social dimensions (foood security).
www.oecd.org.substainabledevelopment

Agriculture: Improving Policy Coherence for Development, OECD Policy Brief (2008):
This Policy Brief explains the importance of agriculture for development and looks at how the OECD is using its multidisciplinary policy expertise and direct contacts in national ministries and authorities to help governments promote policy coherence for development in agriculture.
www.oecd.org/publications/policybriefs

Aid for Trade at a Glance (2007):
This joint OECD/WTO report provides the first comprehensive global picture of aid for trade and will enable the international community to assess what is being achieved, what is not, and where improvements are needed.

Paris Declaration on Aid Effectiveness (2005):
The Paris Declaration is an international agreement to which over 100 Ministers, Heads of Agencies and other Senior Officials committed their countries and organisations to continue to increase efforts in harmonisation, alignment and managing aid for results with a set of monitorable actions and indicators.
www.oecd/org/dac/effectiveness/ parisdeclaration

In April 2006, OECD Environment and Development ministers met to discuss ways of helping developing countries to strengthen their economies without harming the environment. The outcomes of the meeting were a **Framework for Common Action around Shared Goals** and a **Declaration on Integrating Climate Change Adaptation into Development Co-operation**.
www.oecd.org/epocdacmin2006

4

2026

Our world is showing signs of reaching critical thresholds in all of its major systems. Striking a balance between the needs and resources of today and tomorrow poses tough choices. What tools can help us decide how best to manage our systems for the long term?

The Future
Is Now

By way of introduction...

Straddling the border of Poland and Belarus is a magical place, seemingly untouched for thousands of years. In the spring, wildflowers bloom under majestic oaks, and animals give birth to their young in the last remaining fragment of a primeval forest that once covered almost all of western Europe. The preservation of this particular region began centuries ago, when tsars and princes reserved the land as a private hunting ground for the elusive and increasingly rare wisent, the European bison. During the First World War, the forest and its inhabitants were again in serious danger: logging mills were built, and the last wild wisent was killed by a poacher in 1919. It seemed this last corner would go the way of wild areas on the rest of the European continent, with the virgin forest and its large mammals lost forever.

As soon as peace returned, however, determined conservationists went to work, and in 1932 the Bialowieza National Park was established. In the decades since, this unique ecosystem has been recognised as a UNESCO World Heritage Site and Biosphere Reserve. The wisent were reintroduced in 1952 from the small population surviving in zoos. Today, the bison population is healthy at about 250 individuals, in addition to other large mammals such as elk, deer, wolves, wild horses and over 100 species of birds. Each year, 100 000 tourists visit the small area of the forest open to the public, for a glimpse at this rare and wonderful ecosystem.

At the end of 19th century, the primeval forests of western Europe had been gone for generations, and in the United States the last borders of virgin forests were being logged. Species like the American bison had been hunted down to the last few hundred; others like aurochs and the great auk were gone forever. But a movement to protect the last wild places swept across Europe and the Americas, and over the 20th century thousands of square kilometres were set aside, protected in one way or another, for future generations.

By establishing national parks we narrowly escaped the permanent loss of many species and ecosystems. Now we turn to our future and wonder – what is it that we need to protect, or risk losing forever? With economic development and urbanisation racing ahead, how do we ensure that we're giving future generations a fair chance for the kind of lifestyle we've enjoyed? As the pace of human activity and impact increases, today's adults might even worry for the stability of our own future.

A century ago it seemed enough to set aside areas of special habitat. Today, we know that not only have we used up certain resources, accumulated national debt and released long-lasting pollution into water, air and soil, we're even changing the climate on which our lives depend. Clearly, it is time for another type of conservation movement: one that helps us manage what is important to our well-being and that of future generations, responsibly and sustainably.

▶ This chapter looks at the need for forward-looking thinking to achieve sustainable development and the tools available to help this thinking. But it also stresses the need to act now, since many of the issues future generations will have to deal with are already present today, and the more we wait the more difficult it will be to tackle them.

A fair share between generations

> "In addition to balancing economic, environmental and social objectives, a basic tenet of sustainable development is the need to balance the needs of current and future generations."
>
> *Good Practices in the National Sustainable Development Strategies of OECD Countries*

When the concept of sustainable development was first articulated in the Brundtland Report, fairness to future generations was a central tenet. This concept is sometimes called *intergenerational equity*. While relations between nations are regulated with laws and agreements, people who will live in the future can't defend their rights, even though their well-being is affected by our actions. We therefore have a duty to protect their interests, even at the cost of potential short-term gains to us.

The problem is not only one for generations at some far off time disconnected from the present: in reality, the future is as early as the child born five minutes from now. Managing systems for the long term is not an altruistic notion. Our interest is in the future because we are going to spend the rest of our lives there, to paraphrase American inventor Charles Kettering.

This is obviously a huge challenge, involving choices that we as citizens have to inform ourselves about. Take some of the most hotly debated topics such as health, pensions or public debt. You often hear that health expenditures will rise because of population ageing – the "grey dependency ratio" shown in the graph. But analyses carried out by the OECD present a more complicated picture. Although health costs rise with age, the average cost per individual in older age groups should fall over time in part because people are not only living longer, they're staying healthier longer. And they'll be getting pensions longer, too. Should it be up to individuals to make sure they have enough to live on at retirement, or should we tackle this issue as a community? Or what about public debt? Is it merely a burden we're passing on to our children or are the infrastructures, education or other services it pays for an investment in their future?

And what about our stewardship of the earth's land and resources? Outside of those lands set aside for protection, we have a history of exploiting resources through intensive activity. Can we manage most or all our forests, wetlands and oceans so that they continue to provide the riches we rely on? Are the habitat changes caused by our development endangering species that our descendents might value for aesthetic and philosophical reasons, or even practical uses like medicine and agriculture?

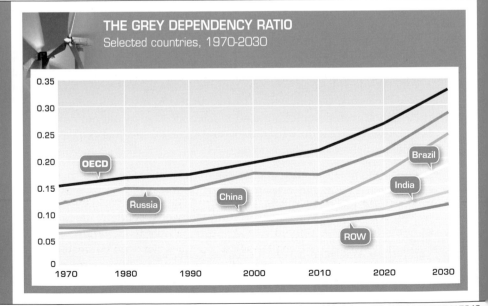

THE GREY DEPENDENCY RATIO
Selected countries, 1970-2030

Source: OECD Environmental Outlook to 2030.   StatLink  : http://dx.doi.org/10.1787/470855417842

OECD Insights: Sustainable Development

It is as if suddenly, after tens of thousands of years of human progress and all the activity that goes with it, we have finally grown into our planet: we can reach its most remote corner; we circle it in a day; we can re-direct its rivers and climb its highest peaks. It also seems that we could soon grow out of it if we do not proceed carefully.

Indeed, the planet is showing signs of reaching critical thresholds in all of its major systems. Climate change, species loss and pollution are evidence that the world's capacity to handle what humans generate is close to full. Lest this sound like a purely "environmental" problem, keep the following in mind: the changes that occur as a result of higher temperatures, natural disasters or losing an important insect in the food chain all have profound effects on individual human beings and society as a whole. If there is one realisation that seems to have taken hold since the advent of sustainable development, it is that the environment, the people who inhabit it, and the economies and cultures they thrive on depend on each other.

> "The remaining environmental challenges are of an increasingly complex or global nature, and their impacts may only become apparent over long timeframes. Among the most urgent of these challenges for both OECD and non-OECD countries are climate change, biodiversity loss, the unsustainable management of water resources and the health impacts of pollution and hazardous chemicals. We are not managing our environment in a sustainable manner."
>
> *OECD Environmental Outlook to 2030*

Learning to be sustainable: what tools do we have?

For over a hundred years, forestry schools have been teaching how to manage forest resources. Knowing how fast a certain species of tree will grow in a given climate, it is possible to calculate the sustainable yield. In a tree plantation, the trees can even be treated as an 80-year agricultural crop with the same species covering thousands of hectares, and they can be harvested indefinitely if the soil is fertilised and climate conditions don't change.

This type of forest, with trees of one age and one species, is not a useful habitat for very many other species, but even tree plantations can be managed for maximum biodiversity.

A bigger challenge today is managing fisheries resources: the main way we have of tracking these populations is based on catch. How can we know whether we're overharvesting the resource? Improvements in equipment and methods engineered over the last half century allow for greater catch – giving the impression at a given point in time that the population is healthier than ever – until it crashes. This is precisely what has happened in some of the world's best fisheries, such as the Grand Banks off the coast of Newfoundland in Canada.

At least one-quarter of marine fish stocks are overharvested. The quantity of fish caught increased until the 1980s but is now declining because of the shortage of stocks. In many sea areas, the total weight of fish available to be captured is less than a tenth of that available before the onset of industrial fishing. Inland fisheries, especially important for providing high-quality diets for the poor, have also declined due to overfishing, changes to habitats and withdrawal of fresh water.

What can be done to conserve these valuable aquatic resources for future generations? Marine biologists, fishermen and policy experts have proposed several possible solutions to make sure that fish stocks will be available well into the future: quotas are imposed for each species, in hopes that enough are left in the waters to reproduce; Marine Protection Areas are established, with strictly no fishing, as a base from which populations can grow. Naturally, these policies are only effective when they are fully enforced. For the fishers themselves, government programmes buy back boats, offer professional reconversion programmes and try generally to support communities where there are simply too many fishers for the resource.

Finally, we can replace wild fish with a more easily-managed resource: fish from aquaculture. Aquaculture currently provides almost 40% of the fish and shellfish we eat, but it has its limits as well. Raising so many fish in such small quarters makes the risk of infection so high that antibiotics have to be used. Escaped fish interbreed with wild populations, endangering their genetic diversity, and pollution from the fish food and wastes flows

The Collapse of the Grand Banks cod fishery

The rich fishing grounds off the southeast coast of Canada have been exploited for hundreds of years, from the 17th century when Basque fisherman ventured north to the late 20th when an estimated 40000 people worked in the fishing industry of Newfoundland, catching and processing cod. During the 1990's the harvest reached a very profitable maximum, before crashing in 1992, for reasons that still aren't fully understood. What we do know is that the collapse is still costing upwards of 250 million Canadian dollars per year in lost income. For local residents in towns like Bonavista (population 4000), other occupations need desperately to be found: the cod population still shows no sign of recovery despite a moratorium on cod fishing enacted in 1994.

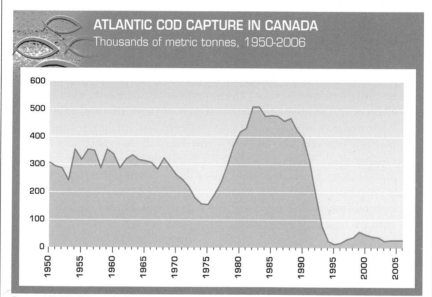

ATLANTIC COD CAPTURE IN CANADA
Thousands of metric tonnes, 1950-2006

Source: UN FAO Fishstat database.

With the end of the cod harvest, people started fishing for skates, which were formerly considered "by-catch". Now evidence shows that the skates too are overfished. Clearly, this is not a sustainable solution, and the local communities are paying the price in lost income and tradition: Bonavista has lost one-tenth of its population over the last decade, turning to tourism as its fishers hope for a miracle.

In the meantime, they have a warning for other fisheries where the catch is still high, "It would be better for them to take drastic measures now, bite the bullet for a little while and then hopefully their stock will rebuild" says Larry Tremblett, a Bonavista fisherman, "Not like what happened to us, just letting it go until there was nothing left. As far as Newfoundland is concerned now, our fishery has gone – wiped out, and all because of greed and stupidity."

easily into surrounding waters. All of these problems will require continued attention and investment in order for aquaculture to become a truly sustainable solution.

With hindsight, the tragedy of Grand Banks seems avoidable. Yet other fisheries are likely in the same situation today as Grand Banks was in 1991, with a catch that seems stable or declining only slowly, but is really nearing or already past its critical threshold. Globally, we still have a very hard time following Larry Tremblett's advice. Even if we know that a crisis may be just around the corner, we all find it difficult to step back and make major changes.

Now is the time to act

One major barrier to making changes is the degree of uncertainty that comes with planning for the future: there is no experiment to "prove" what the exact consequences of unsustainable choices will be. In the case of climate change, we don't know for certain what amount of CO_2 in our atmosphere will trigger serious and possibly irreversible damage – our Earth is our only laboratory on this one. The same is true for biodiversity loss or any of the other resource-management issues that we face. This uncertainty is sometimes taken as an excuse not to make investments in better, cleaner sustainable practices: why pay all that money if we're not *sure* we have to?

And yet that kind of reasoning leaves us vulnerable to a big surprise once there is overwhelming evidence that a systems failure of some type will be devastating, it is likely to be too late to muster the means to avoid it. Sure, some miracle solution might come along, but do we really want to take that risk? What sustainable development argues for is to mitigate those risks now, in ways that enhance our present, as well as preserve our future.

When faced with the prospect of major changes to our environment, a common response is to say "human beings are so resourceful; we'll find a way to deal with that problem when the time comes." Indeed, new methods and technologies can lead to decreased reliance on natural resources, allowing us to give the planet a break, but they can also increase pressure on natural ecosystems or create new worries of their own, as in the fisheries example.

Those technological wonders that we hope will appear in time to save us take years to develop, and there is really no break between a "now" in which we can procrastinate and a "future" when we can start thinking about solutions. Waiting until a problem presents serious consequences is clearly not the best way of managing things.

> **"If no new policy actions are taken, within the next few decades we risk altering the environmental basis for sustained economic prosperity."**
> *OECD Environmental Outlook to 2030*

Even if we can avoid the most drastic outcomes, emergency solutions tend to be very expensive. And often we can only mitigate the negative effects of a problem, rather than erase them. Whether the crisis is starvation, pollution or flooding, those who are affected at the moment of crisis suffer the consequences of a lack of long-term planning. And in the case of species loss, there is no possible solution what is gone is gone forever.

Planning for the future

We want to guarantee that our actions today won't leave behind unsolvable problems and a planet whose capacity to meet the needs of its inhabitants has been depleted. And yet we don't have a crystal ball to look into to see who the people of the future are, how many they are and what resources they require to lead fulfilled lives.

What we *can* do is project into the future using computer models that build on today's situation to try to predict future conditions. Such models can be used to forecast the availability of various social and natural resources, from health care and pensions to fossil fuels and fish. They also forecast the demand for these resources, based on several factors: population growth, economic growth and technology choices. They can give us essential information on what could happen if we do not make the necessary changes.

Imagine possible scenarios for the year 2050: in one, the human population has grown to 9 billion and our societies have continued with fossil fuel-intensive development. As natural gas resources have dwindled coal's share in electricity generation has grown. Increased production has led to increased electricity demand, and more people are driving cars. As a result, annual global greenhouse gas emissions have increased by over 50%, going nearly 47 Gigatonnes – that is, billion tonnes – in 2005 to over 70 Gigatonnes in 2050. The concentration of CO_2 in the atmosphere is above 500 ppm and is still rising.

Another possibility: the same population growth has occurred, but economies have shifted from materials-intensive production to service and information activities. Government policies to mitigate climate change, such as taxing greenhouse gas emissions, have been in place for 40 years. Clean and efficient technologies for generating energy and managing emissions have been rapidly developed and shared worldwide, and non-fossil sources of energy have a far bigger share in the energy mix. Global greenhouse gas emissions peaked around 2015 and the atmospheric concentration of CO_2 is just stabilising at 450 ppm.

These are the kinds of scenarios that policy makers are considering as they try to balance today's needs with tomorrow's: what the world will look like if we change little or nothing, and what we can achieve if we undertake concerted, co-ordinated actions.

Mathematical equations that take into account population, economic growth and energy consumption are used to project future greenhouse gas emissions. This data is then plugged into an even more complex climate model, revealing, with the best current knowledge we have, the impacts. If we're heading towards the first scenario, we could expect a temperature increase of 4-6°C or more in the long term. In the second scenario, the models indicate a more moderate 2-3°C in the long term. Remember that for humans, a heat wave that is just a few degrees warmer than usual can cause thousands more deaths, as Europe experienced in the summer of 2003. Not to mention the more complex effects that warmer temperatures are already having on glaciers and ice caps and sea level.

Such models do not tell us what as yet unforeseen solutions might appear on the horizon, but they can help us understand the possible consequences of decisions we make now. And these days they are sending a clear message: our current path of development is hurtling us towards major changes, changes that will affect almost every aspect of our lives.

Mobile banking: developing countries show the way

Efficient financial services are central to economic development, yet most people in the world don't have a bank account. Even in the US, 10 million households do not have accounts at banks and other mainstream financial institutions. Access to financial services is becoming more important even for the very poor as digitised financial transactions become widespread. In the developing countries, the problem is worse in areas where people might have the means to open an account, but where the banks don't find it worthwhile to build a branch.

The result is that the "unbanked", as they are called, have to pay high fees to intermediaries to send or receive money. This can represent a significant "tax" on the wages of workers who send remittances to their families, especially if they are in another country. People may have to spend hours going to the nearest bank to deposit or withdraw funds. Or they may have to trust their cash to someone going to their home area.

But many if not most people who lack access to a bank do have access to a mobile phone, even if it's not their own. And they are never far from a shop selling top-up cards for the phones. This is the basis for mobile banking. Money can be transferred to the phone and cash picked up from the retailer selling the top-up cards. In more advanced applications, becoming common in South Africa, customers can pay for services using their phones. The next stage being planned is a system as practical as cash machines. In other words, it will allow transactions between people using different telephone operators and different banks if they have an account.

There are plans to link this to microfinance schemes. Until now microfinance operations have been run by organisations dedicated to this purpose. But with the spread of mobile banking, large financial institutions are exploring ways to extend their services to the vast numbers of potential customers usually thought of as unprofitable. In an interview to the *Guardian* newspaper, Alastair Lukies, chief executive of one of the companies promoting the plan, explained their thinking: «One of the things the banks are waking up to now is micro-finance and 'the unbanked' has gone from being a thing you talk about in the corporate and social responsibility paragraph at the end of the annual report to being a fantastically viable market.»

Telecoms analysts Juniper Research back this up, forecasting that mobile banking transactions will soar from 2.7 billion in 2007 to 37 billion by 2011, for a value close to $600 billion, driven by users in developing countries who don't have a bank account or credit card. Other forecasts put the total number of transactions at 62 billion.

Source:

Jupiter Research (2008), "The 'great unbanked' to drive mobile finance market", Juniper Research, 17 June 2008, *www.juniperresearch.com*.

Wray, R. (2008), "Cash in hand: why Africans are banking on the mobile phone", *The Guardian*, 17 June 2008, *www.guardian.co.uk*.

Tackling the 'superstar' issue: climate change and our future

"Scientific evidence shows unequivocal warming of the climate system, and the rate of change is accelerating."

Climate Change: Meeting the Challenge to 2050
(an OECD Policy Brief)

Our species, *Homo sapiens*, has established agriculture, cities, writing and an impressive array of technology during the relatively stable climate of the last 10 000 years, since the end of the last ice age. Now evidence shows that we are changing the very climate we depend on, largely because of our dependence on the fossil fuels (first coal, then oil and natural gas) that made the industrial revolution possible. Energy needs will increase in the foreseeable future, as developed countries continue their economic growth and developing countries race to catch up. If governments around the world stick with current policies, the world's energy needs will be well over 50% higher in 2030 than today, with China and India together accounting for almost half the increase in demand.

We are already paying for historic emissions from developed countries with more frequent heat waves and stronger hurricanes. At the current rate, the Arctic waters will be completely ice free in summer by the middle of this century, possibly within ten years. Seas will continue to rise as the warmer water expands and is joined by melt-water from glaciers and ice caps.

For the last two decades the debate about the seriousness of this threat has raged mounting evidence of substantial alteration to the climate on one side and scepticism on the other, with some people dismissing human-caused climate change altogether. Yet the latest scientific evidence overwhelmingly supports the hypothesis of a climate that is already undergoing change due to human activity.

All of these changes have potentially huge financial and social costs that make inaction seem illogical, short-sighted and even immoral. For example, the Intergovernmental Panel on Climate Change (IPCC) warns that agricultural production in many African countries and regions could be severely compromised by climate variability and change. The area suitable for agriculture, the length of growing seasons and yield potential, particularly along the margins of semi-arid and arid areas, are expected to decrease. This would further adversely affect food security and exacerbate malnutrition in the continent. In some countries, yields from rain-fed agriculture could be reduced by up to 50% by 2020.

On the other hand, recent projections show that costs of reducing carbon emissions will have a minimal effect on global growth. World GDP is projected to double by 2030 and triple by 2050. Stabilising greenhouse gases in the atmosphere at about 450 ppm CO_2 is by all calculations affordable compared to expected economic growth and to the estimates of cost of inaction. The OECD estinated that this stabilisation would cost a small fraction of accumulated wealth worldwide in the comming decades, possibly less than one tenth of a percent of world GDP growth. It is not cheap, but manageable.

Melting glaciers are more than just a change of scenery

Hardly a day goes by that that we don't hear or read something about climate change. Most recently, a report by the United Nations Environment Programme has announced the appearance of a rather significant trend: the earth's glaciers are melting much faster than at any time in the past. Of thirty reference glaciers from which scientists have taken regular measurements since 1980, only one has slightly increased. All the others experienced loss, at an average rate more than double the previous year.

What does the loss of major glaciers mean? For some, it's the change in a familiar landscape or the disappearance of species dependent on the integrity of that landscape that seems unfortunate. Footage of polar bears struggling to move across patchy ice are particularly affecting because we are spectators to the effects of the bears' habitat loss, in real time.

But you don't have to be a naturalist or animal lover to be concerned about glacier melt: the effects on people and economies are multiple. For example, scientists have serious concerns about how much water is being added to already-rising oceans and the impact on currents such as the Gulf Stream that play a large role in global climate. Another impact that only the people downstream from a glacier appreciate fully is their role in providing freshwater: snow at the top freezes and is stored for future use while melting releases fresh water into rivers. In the Himalayas, farmers have started building "artificial glaciers", networks of pipes to capture and channel water from melting snow. In temperate zones, this means that water will be available all through a dry summer. As long as the system functions, what is lost is replaced by what is deposited.

At current rates, that kind of replacement is impossible. Scientists at the World Glacier Monitoring Service describe a dramatic scenario: too much melting will initially cause floods. And if the glaciers shrink too much or disappear, they will no longer be able to serve as natural water storage, resulting in a serious lack of freshwater during dryer seasons. For the millions of people who depend on rivers for water to drink, to grow food and to produce energy, this represents a vital threat.

> **"A window of opportunity to act is now open, but it will not be open for long. We need forward-looking policies today to avoid the high costs of inaction or delayed action over the longer-term."**
>
> OECD Environmental Outlook to 2030

When put in those terms, paying the price to reduce carbon emissions now sounds like a smart choice. Also, the more co-operation there is on a global scale, the lower the costs will be.

Calculating the costs of inaction

The cost of making changes has often been cited as the reason why we have not managed to take more comprehensive action to eliminate bad habits. One difficulty arises in trying to calculate and compare these costs. We are quite used to calculating the cost of something new. Say a factory is contemplating changing to a cleaner production process, adding a filter that will reduce emissions of nitrogen oxides (NO_x): first there is the cost of the new equipment itself. To this must be added the costs of stopping production while the modifications are made and the cost of disposing of the old materials.

Determining the cost of inaction, however, requires bringing together a number of previously separate issues, some of might not be easy to put a price tag on, such as health and quality of life. Particulate matter produced by fires, diesel engines and incinerators, among other sources, is known to cause heart and lung disease, cancer and respiratory ailments: 960 000 premature deaths and 9.6 million "years of life lost" worldwide was the estimated figure for the year 2000. Photochemical smog, a result of several emissions present in dense urban areas (NO_x, CO_2, SO_x, and ground level ozone, O_3) also causes respiratory illness, cardiovascular problems and increased mortality.

So how much is this extra pollution costing society? Missed work days for adults and increased asthma treatment for children both cost money to the local and wider economies. Smog also affects the value of real estate, and the growth of plants. These are complex calculations at the local level. At a national level it is estimated that damages from air pollution in the US range between $71 and $277 billion per year.

MITIGATING CO$_2$'S EFFECT ON CLIMATE
Changes in CO$_2$ concentrations over time, 2000 to 2050

CO$_2$ is a "trace gas", making up less than 1% of the Earth's atmosphere by volume, compared to O$_2$ and N$_2$ (21% and 78% of our atmosphere respectively), but as a greenhouse gas it retains heat close to Earth's surface, leading to climate change.

In the past 150 years, humans have increased the concentration of carbon dioxide in the atmosphere from about 280 parts per million to 385 ppm today, principally through the burning of fossil fuels.

Since there is a lag time between when we emit a molecule of CO$_2$ and when its full effects are felt by our very complex climate, there really is no way to "stop global warming". Instead, experts talk about *mitigation*.

It will be many years before we can even imagine reducing atmospheric CO$_2$ back to historic levels, but we can limit its rise.

The graph below shows where CO$_2$ will be in 2050 for a baseline scenario of action (scenario 1 in this text) compared with an aggressive global effort to keep CO$_2$ below 450 ppm (scenario 2).

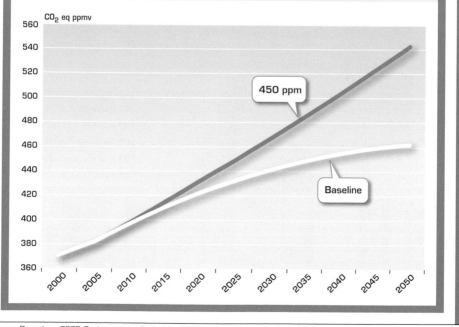

Source: Based on *OECD Environmental Outlook to 2030.* **StatLink** ▤▧ : *http://dx.doi.org/10.1787/470886725475*

Reducing our emissions of greenhouse gases will cost even more than retrofitting factories to control local air pollutants like NO_x. But the potential costs of inaction on climate change are higher, too.

> "We will act with resolve and urgency now to meet our shared and multiple objectives of reducing greenhouse gas emissions, improving the global environment, enhancing energy security and cutting air pollution in conjunction with our vigorous efforts to reduce poverty."
>
> G8 Communiqué, Gleneagles Summit 2005

In response to the political will expressed by leaders of industrialised nations at the G8 Summit at Gleneagles in 2005, the International Energy Agency (IEA) has published a series of scenarios and strategies aimed at meeting environmental goals. The so-called ACT scenarios show that, with the right decisions taken early enough, it is possible to move the energy system onto a more sustainable basis over the next half century, using technologies that are available today or that could become commercially available in the next decade or two. The ACT scenarios only stabilise emissions at 2005 levels.

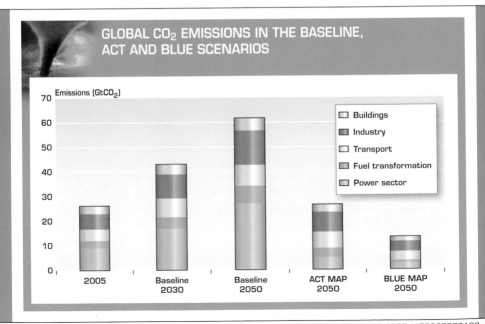

GLOBAL CO_2 EMISSIONS IN THE BASELINE, ACT AND BLUE SCENARIOS

Emissions (GtCO$_2$)

Legend: Buildings, Industry, Transport, Fuel transformation, Power sector

Categories: 2005 | Baseline 2030 | Baseline 2050 | ACT MAP 2050 | BLUE MAP 2050

Source: OECD/IEA (2008), Energy Technology Perspectives 2008: Scenarios and Strategies to 2050.

StatLink : http://dx.doi.org/10.1787/470887573126

But returning emissions to 2005 levels may not be enough. The IPCC has concluded that emissions must be reduced by 50% to 85% by 2050 if global warming is to be confined to between 2°C and 2.4°C. The BLUE scenarios look at how this could be done, including the use of technologies that still have to be developed, such as hydrogen fuel cell vehicles.

Here again, our choices are many: will we combine the forces of governments, the business community and our own personal choices to make the necessary changes? What the scenarios show is that we *are* capable of reducing our emissions, shifting away from activities that affect the climate and still grow our economies *if* we make a concerted international effort to manage the climate change question sustainably.

Educating ourselves for a sustainable future

Finally, we have to take a close look at what got us into our current situation and think seriously about how to change our habits and methods in a way that will last. Now that we know so much more about the relationship between development and the well-being of people and natural systems, we need to find ways to transmit that knowledge.

For future generations to avoid some of the problems we are struggling to solve today, they must continue making better and more sustainable choices. This message is passed on from parents, through the media and increasingly at school: UNESCO declared 2005-2014 the "Decade of Education for Sustainable Development". Nations from Australia to France, from Chile to China, have included environmental concepts in their national curricula and are building eco-schools to ensure that younger generations meet the future with some of the tools they need to carry these ideas forward. But teaching children the complex concepts of sustainable development – interdependency, interdisciplinary thinking, intergenerational needs – is proving far more difficult. Curricula approaches for teaching sustainable development are still at an early stage.

We owe it to future generations to put mechanisms in place to achieve sustainability: nations can start enforcing emissions quotas and trading, to make each ton of CO_2 more expensive to emit, while at the same time developing and sharing alternatives for energy. It is important not to forget that we also owe it to ourselves: many of the consequences may seem like they are in the indefinite future, but that may be much sooner than we would like. Ageing populations, increasing poverty, stronger hurricanes, more frequent heat waves, increased flooding… the evidence suggests that these are no longer projections: the future is now.

Find Out More

On the Internet
For a general introduction to OECD work on sustainable development, visit www.oecd.org/sustainabledevelopment.

Publications

OECD Environmental Outlook to 2030 (2008):
The *OECD Environmental Outlook to 2030* provides analyses of economic and environmental trends to 2030, and simulations of policy actions to address the key challenges. The Outlook shows that tackling the key environmental problems we face today – including climate change, biodiversity loss, water scarcity and the health impacts of pollution – is both achievable and affordable. It highlights a mix of policies that can address these challenges in a cost-effective way. The Outlook reflects developments in both OECD countries and Brazil, Russia, India, Indonesia, China, South Africa, and how they might better co-operate on global and local environmental problem-solving.

Energy Technology Perspectives 2008: Scenarios and Strategies to 2050
IEA, 2008:
This publication responds to the G8 call on the IEA to provide guidance for decision makers on how to bridge the gap between what is happening and what needs to be done in order to build a clean, clever and competitive energy future. The analysis demonstrates that a more sustainable energy future is within our reach, and that technology is the key.

Also of interest

Teaching Sustainable Development (forthcoming 2008):
This report summarises the outcomes of the September 2008 workshop on education and sustainable development and proposes teaching and curricula approaches as an OECD contribution to the UN Decade of Education for Sustainable Development (2005-2014).
www.oecd.org/sustainabledevelopment

Climate Change: Meeting the Challenge to 2050, OECD Policy Brief (2008):
Over the past decade, governments have developed an international framework for action on climate change, and many countries have implemented policies to address it. While this experience will be invaluable as a base for developing future climate policies and a post-2012 framework for tackling climate change internationally, the current actions are insufficient to significantly slow the progress of climate change.
This Policy Brief highlights the OECD's work on the likely impact of various courses of action to mitigate climate change.
www.oecd.org/publications/policybriefs

"The Economics of Climate Change: The Fierce Urgency of Now", Speech by Angel Gurría, OECD Secretary-General, at the UN Climate Change Conference in Bali, Indonesia on 12 December 2007
In his speech, Mr. Gurría presented the climate change policies that should be put into place to limit further deterioration. Answering the crucial question "who pays for it", he noted that the countries who provoked climate change have a greater capacity to pay than those who joined the group of large emitters more recently.
www.oecd.org/secretarygeneral

5

Sustainable development is about making better choices as producers and consumers – choices that do not use up our resources or create consequences that we literally can't live with. To make good choices we have to know something about the products and processes we use on a daily basis. Governments and businesses must work together to make sustainable choices available and more visible to consumers. People need incentives including information and education to begin consuming sustainably.

Production
and Consumption

By way of introduction...

In Samuel Beckett's novel *Malone Dies*, the main character decides to make a list. Taken literally, Malone's idea may seem like a typical example of the absurd. Yet so often with Beckett, an everyday occurrence can suddenly reveal unexpected depths, complexity and connections among what we are, what we do and, in this case, what we have. Imagine trying to write down everything you possess – every single thing. It might take a while, right? Yet go back a few generations and the problem would probably have been a lot easier for most members of your family – food, working clothes, maybe a set of formal clothes that lasted a lifetime, some household utensils and perhaps a few other goods. And that's all.

Even now, the 40% of the world's population living on less than two dollars a day wouldn't need much time to draw up their list of possessions. In OECD countries however, the economic expansion and social reforms of the past few decades have made the material conditions of most people's lives unimaginably superior to those at any other time in history. Rapidly developing economies such as China, India and Brazil are catching up and their consumption patterns are converging with those of OECD countries. Worldwide, more and more people possess more and more things.

This has obvious implications for sustainable development. The billions of goods and components humans now own all have to be manufactured, transported and, sooner or later, disposed of. Consumption and production touch virtually every aspect of our lives: international trade, agriculture, energy, working conditions, social life and well-being. In fact, all the areas considered important to sustainable development actually have something to do with what producers bring to the market and what consumers – whether individuals, groups or governments – take from it.

▶ In this chapter, we'll look at how consumption patterns are changing thanks to more goods being available at prices more of us can afford. We'll also examine the "hidden" costs of production and consumption. And we'll discuss what they mean to the people who have to pay. Finally, we look at what consumers, producers and governments can do to promote more sustainable always of doing things.

The material society

We live in a "productivist" society, where growth and economic activity have long been the central focus of the activities we undertake as individuals and communities. World GDP has grown from around $16 trillion in the mid 1970s to over $40 trillion today. Companies are churning out more of everything and inventing new products all the time.

To take a simple example, let's go back to Malone for minute. He doesn't get very far with his list, overwhelmed as he is by a pencil and a notebook. Even such small and seemingly innocuous objects can give us pause for thought once we begin to add up the totality of their "weight" in the world. Every year, the Faber-Castell company alone produces 2 billion pencils, enough to reach from here to the Moon if laid end to end. An ordinary graphite pencil can write around 45 000 words, that's around 70 closely-written pages, or a line almost 60 km long. So Faber-Castell could probably meet the world's pencil needs for some time to come with a year's output. A quick look at any stationery store tells a different story. The modern marketplace offers an enormous range and quantity of even the simplest products. And manufacturers are continually trying to produce the next big thing, the next hot item that everyone will want. Workers, research, raw materials, machines, components, marketing and distribution, and numerous other services are mobilised to meet our demand as consumers for new and better products.

Although poverty and deprivation still exist, most people in OECD countries enjoy a standard of living that allows them to spend a significant share of their income on goods and services other than food, shelter, clothing or other basics. Even for the basics many of us can spend much more than is necessary for our physical well-being. Consuming is a pervasive fact of life and begins even before babies are born, when the parents' friends and relatives celebrate the big event with a gift. Babies themselves begin to consume, or to influence purchasing decisions, as soon as they can point at a toy or cereal box. In the US for example, discretionary spending by children aged 3 to 11 is expected to grow from $18 billion in 2005 to over $21 billion by 2010, while families will spend over $140 billion on consumer goods for their kids by 2010.

What happened to the paperless office?

Indeed, consumption often seems to be the major criterion in defining activities or social groups. As the chairman of the IFPI, trade association for the recording industry, explained to a trade show in 2005: "A new generation has defined new ways of consuming music". Not "listening to" or "enjoying", but "consuming". In the past few decades, the technology for "consuming" music has undergone several major transformations: records, tapes, CDs and now the immaterial and intangible digital file.

Production has a far greater impact on sustainability than consumption, so taken in isolation, the fact that goods can now be obtained in a digital format is a good thing for sustainability. Selling a million copies of a song via Internet downloads saves tons of plastic, tons of packaging materials and tons of fuel to get the CDs to the shelves and the fans to the store. But, once again, we have to keep in mind that sustainability is not about taking things in isolation, but instead about examining the trends and interactions that make up the whole cycle of production and consumption. In this case, it means remembering that the virtual economy has physical foundations and that the digital product uses resources and creates waste. Over 7 million tons of phones, computers and TVs were sold in 2006, and this is expected to rise to almost 10 million tons a year by 2016. The servers that store all this information are using significant amounts of electricity – over 1% of the world's total.

> Our overriding challenge is to dramatically decouple economic growth from the use of natural resources and degradation of the environment.
>
> Connie Hedegaard, Danish Minister for the Environment,
> *Measuring Subtainable Production*

The digital revolution has added hundreds of new objects to the market and often without the savings in resources that it was assumed the innovations would generate. People have been predicting for the past 30 years that the PC and other advances in electronic equipment would reduce the amount of paper used, leading to the "paperless office". In reality, consumption of paper products has almost tripled since the mid-1970s. Of course not all of this is due to office applications, but the introduction of e-mail into organisations for instance increased paper use by 40%. Other office technologies also have significant sustainability impacts, as in the 3.3 litres of oil it takes to produce a laser printer cartridge. And in spite of the possibilities for savings in travel through telecommuting, the vast majority of people still work in an office, with fewer than 2% of workers working more than eight hours a week at home.

Why has technological progress and the so-called information society not produced the resource (and time) savings that should be possible? Well, for a start, goods have become cheaper – you can now buy a laser printer for the price you would have paid for the cheapest inkjet printers five years ago – and world living standards are rising, increasing the number of buyers of every kind of object. The answer to this question also has to account for how people use the technologies, favouring throw-away objects rather than reusable ones for example. Making production and consumption sustainable means considering the whole life cycle of a product, from the raw materials needed for production to labour costs and conditions, to the costs of transport, retail distribution, use and waste disposal.

Two sides of the same coin

Production and consumption together form the backbone of the economy. They also help to determine social status and shape the natural environment. We can better understand some of these issues by looking at an everyday object, the mobile phone.

Thirty years ago, the idea of a tiny radiotelephone capable of calling practically anywhere in the world was the stuff of futurist fancy. Today, not to have a mobile is to pass for an oddball, or a technophobe. Even in countries where income is very low and poverty a major concern, mobile technology is relatively common, having leapfrogged traditional telecoms in many cases. There are only about 14 fixed-line telephone subscriptions for every 100 people in developing countries, but over 33 mobile subscribers. And the trend for mobiles is moving sharply upward, while that for fixed is actually declining in the developed countries according to the International Telecommunications Union.

What does this mean for sustainable development? It means that more people than ever have access to modern communications networks and the benefits they bring. As Internet via mobile phone expands, it will mean that people who can't afford a computer can access the Web. It means that banking services can be made available without having to build banks. But since we are looking at all that goes into (and comes out of) a product, we have to examine the physical impact of all these phones, too. Worldwide mobile subscriptions had reached 3.3 billion by the end of 2007, and a billion mobile phones are sold each year. An average user changes phones every 18 months to two years and very few of the old ones are recycled. Although one phone may not make much difference, the life cycle of billions of phones is a major issue.

Out of sight, out of mind?

What really happens to all that waste at the end of a product life? What does it mean exactly to "store or reuse" it? Where does it really go when "exported"? In 2006, the tanker *Probo Koala* offloaded a cargo of toxic wastes onto trucks in Abidjan, the Ivory Coast capital. The trucks then dumped the waste at 14 municipal dumps around the city. The resulting pollution killed at least 7 people and poisoned 9 000 others, provoking vomiting, nosebleeds, headache and rashes. The story starts in Amsterdam, where the cost for treatment would have been €500 000. The ship sailed on to Estonia, which refused to let the waste enter its territory. It was then sent it to Africa, and a newly registered company was paid $18 500 to dispose of the

---

Electronic waste

> Nokia looked at how much CO_2 a typical 3G phone generates in a year: 12.3 kg for manufacturing, 33 kg for equipment operating, and 9.6 kg for operator activities, giving a total of almost 55 kg of CO_2 per phone. The study also describes a number of substances that are harmless while the phone is intact, but that could be dangerous if recycling is not carried out correctly (*http://ec.europa.eu/environment*).

> According to the UN, 20 to 50 million tons of waste from electrical and electronic equipment, WEEE, are generated each year from the products we throw away. (In 2005, visitors to London could see the Weee man,

a 7 metre high giant composed of the estimated electrical and electronic waste one UK citizen will discard in a lifetime.) Greenpeace estimates that only 25% of WEEE generated in the EU27 each year is collected and treated. No precise data are available on whether the rest is stored, disposed of otherwise within the EU, or exported to developing countries. Part of the 25% collected may also be exported, and hazardous waste exports are taking place despite an EU ban on such exports to non-OECD countries. Figures for the US are similar, with 80% of this waste incinerated, sent to landfill, put into "storage or reuse", or exported (*www.greenpeace.org*).

---

waste. The *Probo Koala* case is only one example of the "grey areas" involved in disposing of material waste. Like similar cases, it reveals some of the many governance, regulatory and even geopolitical factors that can impede or hinder sustainability.

The raw materials side of a product's life cycle can also have a significant influence on people's quality of life, their health and safety. This can even inadvertently contribute to conflict, as in the case of the capacitors found in phones, laptops and other electronic devices, which use a substance called tantalum, valued for its good thermal conductivity and energy efficiency. Although Australia is the world's biggest producer, the increased demand has made other sources attractive, too. A UN report revealed that the civil war in the Democratic Republic of Congo was being partly financed by illegal mining and trading of coltan, the African abbreviation for columbo-tantalite, a source of tantalum. Phone manufacturers do not buy coltan directly, and knowing which components suppliers are using illegal materials is extremely difficult, the more so given the sheer number of components that go into a phone – 500 to 1 000 depending on the model.

Getting the price right

If asked to describe how the price of goods is fixed, most of us could describe the various factors taken into account, such as raw materials, labour, profit margins and so on. But these economic parameters do not tell the whole story. The *Economist* magazine has devised an amusing and instructive index it calls the Big Mac index to compare prices around the world. For example, an average American would have to work for around ten minutes to buy a hamburger, while a Kenyan would have to work for three hours. We can use this novel way of looking at things to think about production and consumption.

Most of us wouldn't mind working 10 or 15 minutes to buy a hamburger. But what if you had to find the 2 400 litres of water needed to make it? You are probably familiar with the idea of carbon footprints – the amount of CO_2 generated by various activities such as travel. The water footprint is a similar figure calculated for the use of fresh water. It is based on the idea of "virtual water". A tee-shirt for example contains no water, but it takes 11 000 litres on average to produce a kilogram of the cotton it's made of, once you include irrigation, bleaching, dyeing and all the other steps in

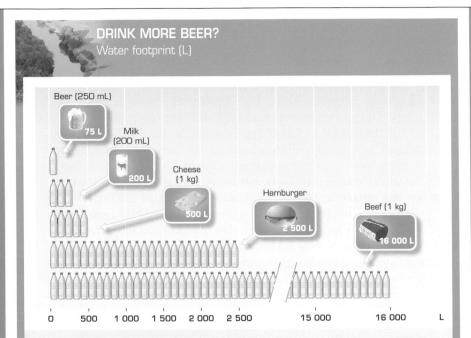

DRINK MORE BEER?
Water footprint (L)

The water footprint of an individual is the total water used for the production of the goods and services he or she consumes.

Some products you might think are similar to each other show surprising variations. A cup of tea "costs" 30 litres of water for instance, while coffee costs 140 and fruit juice 190.

You could argue that drinking beer is the righteous path for the concerned citizen since a 250 ml glass will only set the planet back 75 litres of water. But as pointed out above, the water footprint includes the whole production chain, and the can, bottle or barrel has to be included, too. The global average water footprint of industrial products is 80 litres per dollar of value added, but this varies widely, *e.g.* 10 to 15 litres for Japan, Australia and Canada; 20 to 25 for India and China; and 50 for Germany and the Netherlands. The water footprint of a nation includes that part of the footprint that falls inside the country (internal footprint) and the part due to using water in other countries (external footprint). The global average per person is about 1 250 m³ a year, half the value of the biggest per capita consumer, the US. For China, it is 700 m³ of which only about 7% is outside the country. Japan, with a footprint of 1 150 m³, has about 65% of its total water footprint abroad.

the production chain. Virtual water is therefore the total amount used to make a product, adding up to 2 700 litres for a shirt. Unlike the fuel that produces CO_2 though, water is rarely sold at a price to the main users that takes into account all the costs incurred. Often the costs of providing infrastructure, purification, waste treatment and distribution are subsidised, so there is less incentive to use water sustainably.

What's the real price and who pays?

Economists use the term externalities to describe the positive and negative aspects not accounted for directly in prices. Bees are often cited as a typical positive externality. The beekeeper raises them to be able to sell honey, but they pollinate all the plants in the area, providing a benefit to farmers and gardeners. Pollution from factories is a typical negative externality where the cost to public health is not included in the productions costs the polluters pay. Getting the price right means getting closer to the "real" price – and this requires factoring in what the production and the consumption of something will generate in terms of externalities.

Assigning a value to things that previously fell outside systems of accounting, budgeting and measurement is a major challenge. It is not easy, for example, to assign a value to natural resources. For some, such as forests, we can calculate the value of what is produced because it is bought and sold and therefore has a monetary value. Still, knowing the price of wood – and therefore knowing something about what a forest is worth monetarily – doesn't tell us anything about its value in offsetting CO_2 emissions, its role in preserving biodiversity or its spiritual and cultural value to people whose way of life depends on it. Assigning a value to clean air is harder still. Air pollution generates costs in the form of increased rates of disease, lower real estate values in "dirty" areas, and current and future damages related to climate change. Clean air is worth something to us, but can we say how much exactly? The "ecological services" concept sees that putting a price on these services is a useful way for them to be valued – getting the "real cost" of resource consumption into the equation.

In the meantime, nearly two-thirds of the services provided by nature to humankind were found to be in decline worldwide by the UN's Millennium Ecosystem Assessment. The UN points out that the costs may be borne by people far away from those enjoying the benefits, as when shrimp eaten in Europe is farmed in a South Asian pond built in place of mangrove swamps – weakening a natural barrier to the sea and making coastal communities more vulnerable.

Current trends in global production and consumption patterns are unlikely to change significantly, meaning that externalities will increase. Goods are becoming cheaper and are being transported in ever-bigger amounts from one side of the world to the other. Even a simple pot of yoghurt may have travelled over 3 000 km by the time it reaches the table and require inputs from several countries for its ingredients, production and packaging. We replace goods much more quickly than in the past. Few people still use an MP3 player they bought five years ago, for instance, but an old gramophone would have lasted for decades. And unlike our grandparents' generation, we throw out rather than repair everything from vacuum cleaners to socks.

Corporate social responsibility

The idea behind corporate social responsibility – that corporations have an obligation to consider the impact of their activities on the environment, economy and society – is not exactly new. How companies treat their employees and what kinds of products they submit to their customers has been the topic of debate for centuries.

In its contemporary version, corporate social responsibility can encompass everything from service to shareholders, community, governance, diversity, employees, environment, and human rights. A big part is reporting – letting the public and shareholders know about what the companies are doing to fulfil their role as corporate citizens. This is also a way for corporations to communicate their "good deeds" for public relations purposes. Third-party organisations also produce "report cards" rating corporations on the different aspects of social responsibility.

The benefits of increased corporate responsibility are clear, but there may also be more ambiguous issues.

Corporate power may also increase along with responsibility. Corporate social responsibility allows companies to publicise their good actions but can also obscure unsustainable practices in other areas, especially in the case of multinationals with complex supply chains and subcontractors that may or may not be following company guidelines. The problem with corporate social responsibility, as promoted in the OECD Guidelines for Multinational Enterprises, is that it is voluntary. In some cases, corporations are out in front of governments in terms of addressing climate change and other problems. But the time is coming when companies will be required by governments to fulfil their environmental and social obligations both at home and abroad in the interest of sustainable development.
www.oecd.org/daf/investment/cr.

Technology might reduce some of the negative impacts on sustainability of production and consumption but it will create others, and technological improvements are often outpaced by growth in consumption. Cars are now much more fuel-efficient than before, for instance, but air pollution is getting worse because so many more people have cars.

While market-related transactions have grown ever more efficient and many private goods such as food, cars, air-conditioning and designer clothes can, in principle, be afforded by anyone who would like them, the growing externalities of these transactions has made many "public" goods increasingly scarce: clean air, silence, clear space, clean water, splendid views, and wildlife diversity are highly valued and sought after. Nearly every transaction of private goods carries an invisible cost, paid by everyone through degraded public goods. Achieving "decoupling" between continued economic growth and prosperity and the negative externalities created by such development is therefore a major challenge for achieving "development that lasts".

What do cheap clothes really cost?

The way products are produced and consumed affects not just the environment, but also living and working conditions. Once again, looking at an everyday object can help us understand the issues. Fred Pearce, *New Scientist's* senior environment correspondent, set out to discover where the cheap pair of jeans he bought in London came from. His investigation took him to Dhaka, the capital of Bangladesh, where hundreds of thousands of women make clothes for the big brands of Europe and North America – for just under one dollar for a ten-hour day. On his blog and in the book he wrote afterwards, Pearce reports that the companies behind these brands say they insist on decent conditions for the workers. But the women point out that the sociologists who conduct the regular "social audits" of factory conditions do not learn the truth: before they come, "the managers instruct us what to say about working hours and holidays and conditions".

> "Advancing on sustainability concerns fuller attention to the role of the workforce in helping attain the triple bottom line – maximising profits, people and the planet."
> Roland Schneider, Trade Union Advisory Committee to the OECD,
> *Measuring Subtainable Production*

Does this sound unfair? It might come as a surprise to learn that none of the women Pearce spoke to supported boycotts of the goods they make. As he points out, they are the first women in conservative, rural Bangladesh to have any sort of freedoms beyond those allowed by their husbands in the villages. "The garments industry has created a revolution in women's economic empowerment," says Mashuda Khatun Shefali, who runs an NGO that supports women garment workers and tries to improve their conditions. Another campaigner, Nazma Akter, notes that, poor as most were, "women are becoming an economic force here. This is the first time they have had jobs. They are independent now. They can come and go; nobody stops them. Don't take that away from them."

What these women ask from consumers in the rich countries is to pay a fair price for the goods they make and not to ask them to sacrifice their health and well-being for a marginal improvement in our standard of living. Women's status, workers' rights and fairer trade are as much a part of sustainable development as protecting the environment. Making production and consumption sustainable implies recognising the true costs of what we make and what we buy, across the entire supply chain, from sourcing to retail distribution to waste disposal.

Connecting the dots

What can be done concretely to promote sustainable production and consumption? Even quite small actions can have a large cumulative impact. According to the US Environmental Protection Agency, if every home in America replaced just one incandescent light bulb with a compact fluorescent one, in one year enough energy would be saved to light more than 3 million homes and prevent greenhouse gas emissions equivalent to those of more than 800 000 cars.

Or, as the European Lamp Companies Federation calculated, if Europeans switched to the more efficient bulbs, the continent would need 27 fewer power plants. This trade association has launched an effort to encourage European consumers to switch to the energy-saving bulb. Australia, Japan and the state of California plan to implement bans on incandescents, seeing the need for government to step in and make the switch more rapid and definitive. The European Commission is talking about a phase-out, too.

Most successful efforts at influencing markets involve co-ordinated efforts – where producers, consumers and governments each have a role to play. Only through the combination of these efforts can old behaviours and processes be transformed on a large enough scale to make sustainable development the rule rather than the exception.

Co-ordinating our efforts

How can producers integrate sustainability into product design, manufacture and distribution without sacrificing traditional factors such as profit or brand image? We can't really be sustainable consumers without sustainable product choices.

Design is arguably the most influential single stage in the process, since it determines the rest. First of all, the design has to consider the product as part of a product system and consumer lifestyle. If a phone integrates a camera and an MP3 player, will users then buy only the phone, saving the environmental and other costs of manufacturing three separate products? Or will they also buy the others, adding

---

Read this and save over €500 year!

An argument commonly heard against sustainable development is that whatever benefits it brings, it costs too much and would somehow reduce our standard of living. In fact, the opposite can be true.

Energy-saving technologies can save you money, although the savings tend to be in the long run and require the initial investment such as in a fuel pump, improved windows or a hybrid car. On the other hand, unsustainable consumption can cost an astonishing amount, although we may not be aware of just how much. For example, people living in Britain throw away around a third of the food they buy. Most of it (4.1 million tons a year) could have been eaten. The most common reason for food being wasted is that it's simply isn't eaten – 61% of the avoidable food waste or 2.5 million tons. Of this, almost 1 million tons isn't even touched, and at least a tenth –

340000 tonnes – hasn't passed its "use by" date. Cooking and preparing too much results in an additional 1.6 million tons of food waste a year.

It costs UK local authorities £1 billion (around €1.3 billion) to collect and send most of this wasted food to landfill. Stopping the waste of good food could avoid 18 million tons of CO_2 being emitted each year, the equivalent of taking one in five cars off the road.

And the 500+ we said you'd save? Uneaten food costs people in the UK £10 billion every year, that's an average of £420 per household, or over €500 you could save by better planning, storage and management.

See "The food we waste" at
www.wrap.org.uk.

---

to the burden? Design also means choosing the materials from which the product will be made. Can the product be designed in such a way as to maintain the required physical properties while using fewer materials? Could it be made of renewable, recyclable materials? Design also influences manufacturing by determining the number of steps in the production process.

> **"In order to incorporate sustainability management, companies need to work in partnership with other organizations and groups, which have an interest in the company's activities and their economic, social and environmental impacts."**
> Rajesh Kumar Singh, Bhilai Steel, India, *Measuring Subtainable Production*

Questions specific to manufacturing can involve how to reduce energy consumption or pollution, or how to improve worker safety. Once the product is made, what is the most sustainable way to package it for shipping and sale? Should it be transported by air, sea or land, by rail or truck?

Design and manufacturing play a big part in determining how long something will last, how many other products it will need to work (*e.g.* batteries) and if it can be repaired or maintained. And finally, producers also have to think about what happens to the product at the end of its cycle. Once again, good design can make a difference. Are the materials used easy and safe to recycle for example? Can parts of the product be refurbished and reused?

Is the customer always right?

Think of your first major purchase – maybe your first bike or a car. Think of all the factors that went into that decision. Cost was probably one of them but so were colour, texture, brand, and a whole host of aesthetic and emotional associations that attract us to the objects we buy. Businesses spend a lot of money on market research and advertising (over $650 billion a year worldwide on marketing alone), trying to understand those associations, to be able to predict and influence people's tastes and preferences.

At first glance, the pervasive influence of marketing and the push to consume seems to be at odds with sustainable consumption after all, unchecked consumption has played a big part in creating many of the problems we currently face. And yet, if we don't know of a less-polluting product for cleaning the kitchen sink or the difference in energy use for an appliance, then we can't make a better decision. Including a sustainability dimension in marketing and distribution allows us to add another, very important criterion to purchasing decisions. It provides information to consumers and is of course a means to influence them in a "sustainable" direction.

Experience of the past decades has shown that providing sustainable products to the niche market of "green" or "fairtrade" consumers is not enough to change patterns on a larger scale, although it has been a significant factor in pushing both producers and consumers in a new direction. The proliferation of eco and fairtrade labels in the last ten years is evidence of that evolution. For a long time, products such as organics and fairtrade suffered from their reputation as "specialty" items, attractive only to a small category of consumers willing to pay extra to consume according to their beliefs. But this trend has started to change, for several reasons.

For one, more people are aware of the impact that their choices have on the world around them. Problems related to unsustainable consumption – the cost of petrol, for example – have become more "real" and have begun to touch the average consumer in more concrete ways. As a result, a growing number of consumers are beginning to ask important questions about what they buy; how much waste is created by the product and its packaging; how much water, energy and other resources go into its production (and into

---

Fairtrade

In 2008, the OECD staff canteen announced that all its hot beverages would come exclusively from Fairtrade sources. The Fairtrade Labelling Organisations (FLO) are seeking sustainable development through trade, giving small farmers and workers in poor countries a "living wage" for their products. The question is why consumers – rather than governments or large firms – are driving the movement to sustainable trade. Consumers are demanding that imported goods are produced in a way that is environmentally and socially sustainable.

The Fairtrade network now reaches 58 developing countries and 1.4 million famers, who are guaranteed a minimum price, a long-term contract and premiums to put towards community development projects. Production must follow certain social standards (worker rights) and environmental standards. In some European countries, Fairtrade now has 20% of the coffee market and over 50% of banana sales. According to its founders, "*Fairtrade is not only about social and environmentally friendly production methods, but about the empowerment and development of producers.*"

---

its disposal); and what are the living and working conditions of the people who produce the goods.

Second, the products themselves have become more mainstream. A wide range of companies are using the tools of marketing to give products and services considered sustainable a cool or sexy identity. Manufacturers are designing more products that are appealing for their aesthetic qualities or their ease of use *as well as* for their environmental and social sustainability – a look at the latest fuel-efficient car designs provides a good example. Most major retail grocery chains now offer a selection of certified "environmentally friendly" products whose market shares are increasing: for instance organic coffee imports to North America grew by 29% over 2006-2007 compared with 2% for conventional coffee.

The changes in consumer awareness and the proliferation of more sustainable products and services seen over the past few years are encouraging. Some critics and consumer advocates rightly point out that some of this is "fluff" or "greenwashing". Products that claim to be environmentally friendly can look much less so once you take a hard look at the list of ingredients or analyse the entire product life cycle. Buying fairtrade coffee cannot alone solve the problem of poverty. While this may be true, it doesn't detract from the fact that sustainable consumption and production are critical to the success of any kind of sustainable development. The fact that more people and businesses recognise and even wish to capitalise on this realisation can be seen as testament to the growing mass appeal of sustainability. Efforts at making the consumer society sustainable are gaining momentum.

What's the government doing about it?

Finding the right policy tools to encourage good production and consumption practices and avoid overlap and inconsistency is one of the biggest challenges that governments face. Elected officials are under pressure from constituents and special interest groups to respond to issues perceived as important and follow a given line of action. For one, decisions must be based on thorough research and sound evidence, or they risk not solving the problems at all and often create additional ones. Governments have the enormous advantage however of being able to make laws and impose regulations. One solution at their disposal is simply to outlaw products and behaviours that are seen to be doing more harm than good. This is what happened to CFCs (gases used in refrigerators and aerosol sprays) that were damaging the ozone layer. The *Montreal Protocol on Substances that Deplete the Ozone Layer* came into force in 1989, and 191 countries have now signed it. Since then, atmospheric concentrations of the most important CFCs and other related gases have either levelled off or decreased. The plastic shopping bag is another example. Bangladesh banned them in 2002 following a movement that began in the 1980s in Dhaka. Discarded bags were blocking drains during the monsoon, causing flooding.

Critics of such plans point out that packaging is a much bigger source of waste than plastic bags. Retailers should be using their buying power to influence packaging choices from their suppliers and governments should be using their regulatory powers, rather than passing off the responsibility for reducing waste to consumers alone. This kind of argument is heard often in discussions around sustainable development: who is primarily responsible for changing bad practices? Where is the best place to focus our efforts? One might counter that, in the above case, why not do it all? Encourage customers to reduce needless use of plastic bags by charging for them, a measure that has shown consistent results. At the same time, encourage retailers to use their influence to reduce packaging and to implement any other measures to curb resource use and waste. And develop government standards for sustainable and recyclable packaging. The town of Modbury in England shows what could be done. The town became the first in Europe to ban plastic bags after shopkeepers agreed to the move following a few weeks campaigning initiated by Rebecca Hosking in the pub one evening. And as she explained to the *Guardian* newspaper, Modbury is a town "… that's always been very conservative. If we've done it, it proves you don't have to be one of those 'green' towns to change over."

The fact is that often, although we might see what would help, changing things is a different story. As former UK Environment minister Margaret Beckett points out, *"Many unsustainable behaviours are locked-in and made 'normal', not just by the way that we produce and consume, but by the absence of easy alternatives"*. Creating those alternatives is thus a priority, one that can benefit from the force of government intervention. The European Union launched an Integrated Product Policy pilot project involving mobile phone producers, component manufacturers, telecoms operators, consumer groups, recyclers, NGOs, government representatives and researchers. A number of governments are making efforts to promote recycling through initiatives such as France's "éco-participation", a surcharge on electronics goods of €0.52 per kilo that goes towards paying recycling costs.

As the CFC example suggests, persuading producers and consumers to change is not always the most efficient way to tackle the issues, nor is it enough to produce a big enough change on a large enough scale. The individual producer or consumer generally has little power to change things or interest in doing so. A manufacturer who decided to go it alone and implement stricter environmental standards or much better pay and working conditions than competitors would be at a considerable disadvantage. People have a hard time reducing their consumption even of products they know are damaging their own health or adopting behaviours that would improve it. Although consciousness about sustainability is improving, waiting for a change of attitude is not the best policy.

Powerful persuaders

Governments have powerful persuaders at their disposal: regulations and taxes. These have long been applied to economic and social policy. Can they work for sustainable development? The answer is yes. Governments originally tried persuasion and communications campaigns to get consumers to use less energy in their homes. They worked with producers to put labels on appliances indicating their relative energy consumption. In the end, they enacted minimum energy efficiency standards, which forced companies to change the design of their products. Although consumers can have some influence, regulating processes and products is the fastest way to sustainable production.

Experience also shows that environmentally related taxes ("green" or "ecotaxes") and emissions trading can be efficient instruments. They can force polluters (whether producers or consumers) to take into account the costs of pollution and can help to reduce the demand for harmful products. Ireland's 2002 "plastax" led to a 90% reduction in the use of plastic bags.

The 1990 the United States Clean Air Act pioneered emissions trading. It included a requirement for a major reduction in sulphur dioxide (SO_2) and nitrogen oxides by 2010. Each polluter had the "right" to emit a certain quantity of SO_2. If they managed to emit less they could keep their permit or sell it; if they emitted more they had to buy quotas from another polluter (or pay a fine greater than the cost of the quota). By controlling the number of quotas allotted, the Environmental Protection Agency has already brought emissions down 50%. Other countries have since started emissions trading schemes.

All OECD member countries now apply several environmentally related taxes (375 in all plus around 250 environmentally related fees and charges). The taxes raise revenues of about 2% to 2.5% of GDP, with 90% of this revenue from taxes on motor vehicle fuels and motor vehicles.

The environmental effectiveness and economic efficiency of green taxes could be improved if existing exemptions and other special provisions were scaled back or if the rates were made highly dissuasive. The rise in fuel prices shows that cost can be a big factor in changing behaviour, but the level of carbon taxes is generally too low to make it worthwhile for manufacturers to change production methods. Moreover, higher tax rates can face political opposition for two reasons. First is the fear of reduced international competitiveness in the most polluting sectors of the economy. This is why the taxes are levied almost exclusively on households and the transport sector, leaving energy-intensive industries totally or partially exempt. Second, exemptions create inefficiencies in pollution abatement and are contrary to the OECD's "polluter pays" principle.

Another point to bear in mind is that, in practice, environmentally related taxes are seldom used in complete isolation. A labelling system for instance can help increase the effectiveness of a tax by providing better information to the users. Combining a tax on energy use with subsidies or government standards for better isolation of buildings can be a good way to encourage energy savings. The combination of a tax and a voluntary approach can increase the political acceptability of the tax, although this may reduce environmental effectiveness or increase the economic burdens placed on other groups.

What's next?

Seeing, calculating and understanding exactly what we buy, use and waste is just a beginning. It's an important first step in gaining awareness, but it would be unfortunate and ineffective if tools like the footprint are used only as gadgets. Realising that it takes x amount of water or oil to make a given thing has to lead us to at least two questions:

> ➤ How could we develop more efficient processes that are implemented on a large scale – in order to significantly reduce resource use and the negative impacts of production?

> ➤ How should we use the role of "informed consumers" to make sustainable consumption decisions on a scale that produces real results?

As we said at the beginning of this chapter, production and consumption are at the heart of sustainability. From a material point of view, life today is far better than it was a century ago for most people. If the improvement is to continue and benefit the world's population as a whole, the economic, social and environmental pillars of sustainability will have to be reconciled. This will not be easy. Sometimes what might favour one pillar will damage another. Different social groups will have different priorities and projects. But debating these differences and finding solutions is not beyond us, in fact it's what democracy does. This will be discussed in the final chapter which looks at how governments, civil society and business could work together in creating the incentives, rules and regulations that make sustainable development possible.

Find Out More

On the Internet

For a general introduction to OECD work on sustainable production and consumption, visit *www.oecd.org/sustainabledevelopment* and *www.oecd.org/env/cpe*.

Publications

Measuring Sustainable Production (2008): Most people support sustainable development without knowing what it is. What exactly are sustainable consumption and sustainable production, and how are these practices identified? This book reviews the state-of-the-art in measuring sustainable production processes in industry. It includes types of measurement developed by business, trade unions, academics and NGOs, as well as by the OECD and International Energy Agency.

The Political Economy of Environmentally Related Taxes (2006): Environmentally related taxes are increasingly used in OECD countries, and there is ample and increasing evidence of their effectiveness. However, there is a high potential for wider use, provided that they are well designed and that their potential impact on international competitiveness and income distribution are properly addressed. Based on experience in OECD countries, this book provides a comprehensive discussion of the issues and of research on the environmental and economic impacts of applying environmentally related taxes.

OECD Guidelines for Multinational Enterprises, Revision 2000
The *OECD Guidelines for Multinational Enterprises* were adopted by OECD member governments plus Argentina, Brazil and Chile in June 2000. This booklet comprises the revised text and commentary, implementation procedures and the Declaration on International Investment and Multinational Enterprises.

Also of interest

Promoting Sustainable Consumption: Good Practices in OECD Countries (2008): This report highlights OECD government initiatives to promote sustainable consumption, with an emphasis on individual policy tools and instruments and their effective combination.
www.oecd.org/sustainabledevelopment.

UN Millennium Ecosystem Assessment (*www.millenniumassessment.org*): This report assesses the consequences of ecosystem change for human well-being. It provides a scientific appraisal of the condition and trends in the world's ecosystems as well as the basis for action to conserve and use them sustainably.

Toxic Tech: Not in Our backyard, Greenpeace 2008: (*www.greenpeace.org*): This report investigates the global sales of electrical and electronic products and assesses the amount of resulting waste.

The Water Footprint (*www.waterfootprint.org*): This website is maintained by the University of Twente in collaboration with the UNESCO-IHE Institute for Water Education, the Netherlands.

The Food we Waste (*www.wrap.org.uk*): The Waste & Resources Action Programme is working to ensure that the UK reduces waste and recycles as much as possible at minimum net cost.

6

Meeting today's and tomorrow's needs requires knowing what we have, what we consume, what will remain and what can be regenerated or replaced. Accurate measurements and accounting of our natural, social and economic capital are essential to moving forward on a sustainable path.

Measuring Sustainability

By way of introduction...

The previous pages explored what sustainable development means and how contemporary societies are trying to implement it. But how do we know if what we're doing is helping or hurting, or having no effect at all? How do we know that one way of doing or making things is more sustainable than another? That a city, region or country is doing well in terms of sustainable development? How do we calculate today's needs and measure our progress in meeting them? And how can we get some idea of how our decisions will affect the future our own and our children's? To be able to answer these questions, we have to decide first on the basics. What is important to us? What resources do we need to keep track of? What are the different factors that contribute to our quality of life and well-being?

We often have to do this kind of calculation in our daily lives. We know how much money we have and how much we need to buy food and pay the bills. We know, albeit imperfectly, what expenses we'll have to meet later, and we know that there will probably be some unexpected ones, too. We know what we'd like to do and if there is something left over we can spend it on dinner and a movie, clothes or maybe even a holiday. All this depends on counting, planning and reasonable guesses. It is based on measuring our "resources" and following what happens to them, establishing priorities among all the things we have to do and those we'd like to do, sometimes leading to difficult choices. To put it another way, we all have an information system (however informal) to let us see how we're doing just now, make predictions about what we will be able to do in the future, and monitor whether or not we are living within our means.

What makes a good and sustainable society and how can we judge our progress towards creating one? It's more than money, to be sure. The answer lies in a range of factors that make significant, often essential contributions to our "success" from access to education, health care and functioning ecosystems to freedom, justice and cultural expression. Developing and refining accurate measures of these things will allow us to build a more sophisticated and stronger knowledge base, and potentially to speed up progress towards achieving them.

What problems can we not afford to ignore? Like the inhabitants of Rapa Nui mentioned in the first chapter, we depend on systems that are vulnerable to natural and human pressures and linked by a complex web of interactions. Ignorance of the facts critical to our progress, well-being and survival puts us too at risk of encountering undesirable changes that could prove irreversible. The debate continues on the best way of measuring sustainable development in order to provide more precise accounting of whether or not our policies and practices are assuring our longer-term well-being.

▶ This chapter looks at the different tools and criteria used to assess sustainability and how they are combined to provide information on the issues, trends and interactions that determine whether a given situation meets our expectations and what can be done to improve it. It explores which indicators to use to measure sustainable development and how to combine and present them.

Measuring sustainability: what should we count and when?

Agreeing on the best indicators to measure sustainability or progress towards sustainable development is a challenge. An indicator is a summary measure that provides information on the state of, or change in, a system. Indicators give us a snapshot of how we are doing at a given point in time relative to what we've decided is important. Indicators also provide feedback on the effects of our actions and government policies. And indicators have to be able to adapt to the changing conditions and the content of policy.

At first sight, measuring sustainable development seems impossible, the subject is so vast and the influences so many – climate change and child care, business ethics, government policy and consumer trends to name but a few. We know that sustainable development involves economic, social and environmental variables – all of which must be measured to some extent. As shown in the annual *OECD Factbook*, there exist a wealth of indicators from traditional macroeconomic measures, such as gross national product (GNP) and productivity, to environmental indicators, such as water consumption and polluting emissions, and social statistics, such as life expectancy and educational attainment. But which indicators are the most important to sustainable development?

The issue is made even more difficult by the fact that as well as being multidimensional, sustainable development is a dynamic concept. Quantifying it requires juggling a number of parameters including time horizons. Economic, social and environmental phenomena operate at different rhythms to each other (and even within any one of these, several time scales may be operating simultaneously). For instance, the legal systems of most countries are still strongly marked by codes dating from the time of Augustus and the Roman Empire, and their basic principles change slowly. Some technologies, on the other hand, change at a rapid pace your new computer is probably out of date before it's out of the box.

Consider the economy: if you're planning a major energy project, you have to think at least 50 years ahead, but if you're trading on financial markets, the nanoseconds it takes price data to go from one exchange to another can mean substantial gains or losses. For its part, the environment shows how the pace of change can suddenly accelerate, as when fish stocks rapidly disappear after declining slowly for years.

Moreover, we have to bear in mind that sustainable development is a process linking what happened in the past to what we're doing now, which in turn influences the options and outcomes of the future. In a sense, it's like walking along a path backwards – you can see where you've come from, you can see more or less where you are, and you can get a rough idea of where you're heading. But you can't tell if the other paths branching off from your route are dead ends, short cuts or ultimately heading in a completely new direction. Likewise, it's difficult, if not impossible, to say if any given point along the development path is sustainable, it may be more or less so depending on how far we've come, what happens next, which new perspectives open up, and how attitudes and other influences change.

These uncertainties complicate sustainable development measurement. And developing measures is not a purely statistical or technical exercise. It touches on two very sensitive areas for all societies: government accountability and social participation. Measuring progress on sustainable development (or any other important area of policy) with reliable information is a key ingredient of the democratic process. It makes governments more accountable and gives people a tool to participate more actively in defining and assessing policy goals.

Measuring progress

"By measuring progress, we foster progress."

Enrico Giovannini, OECD Chief Statistician

Progress has long been defined and measured in purely economic terms. A country's overall performance or well-being is often expressed in a kind of shorthand fashion through one "superstar" measure: gross domestic product. GDP calculates in monetary terms the value of what counts as production. You may also be familiar with GDP per capita, how much each person in the country would have if everybody got an equal share of GDP. While these measurements may sound fairly straightforward, they omit important factors and include others that we would probably rather live without.

For instance, software that is sold goes into the calculation, but freeware does not. On the other hand, spending on cleaning up an oil spill is included in GDP. In this case, not only is something negative being counted as contribution to "production", but substantial costs to well-being are left out of the equation and remain invisible. Housework, caring for one's children and volunteer work are not counted, though they contribute value to the economy and our daily lives. Per capita GDP is a fairly crude measure, too. As an average, it does not address issues of distribution benefits of economic productivity may go disproportionately to only a small percentage of a population, even though the average looks good.

Such indicators are useful for giving a rough idea of what's happening in the economy and comparing national performance. But there is a large and growing gap between what official statistics, like GDP, tell us about "progress" and what people experience and care about in their daily lives purchasing power, public services, quality of life and so on. The notion that the three pillars of sustainable development should be considered equally important, interconnected and interdependent reflects the idea that economic progress alone is not enough to guarantee that a society is "headed in the right direction". Other factors, such as access to good health care and education, can be equally or more important to creating well-being, life satisfaction and health over the long term, both for the current and the future generations.

> "We cannot face the challenges of the future with the tools of the past."
>
> José Manuel Barroso, European Commission President
> at the international conference on Beyond GDP:
> Measuring progress, true wealth and the well-being of nations,
> 19-20 November 2007

Individual calculations can help us gain awareness of the progress we are making in terms of income or health for example. But if these calculations don't fit within some kind of framework that structures the analysis, we can't get any sense of how we are doing or where we are headed. We need something that allows us to understand the big picture emerging from the data and use it as the basis for policy and action. A conceptual framework can help us select those indicators which best measure what we want to assess in a coherent and consistent manner. It will also help compare sustainability across different societal levels.

Finding ways to make comparisons between countries or regions who may not share the same history, culture, level of economic and social development or physical conditions is a challenge. Reaching this goal requires an ongoing dialogue on needs, resources and how they are evolving, as well as a flexible approach to building sets of indicators that can supply the most useful evidence and information. Individual indicators are the basic building blocks of this process.

The task is complicated further by the fact that what is considered important to sustainability varies to some degree from place to place the quality of water, land or air; people's income or access to energy; life expectancy or any number of other indicators. How then do we develop methods for measurement that reflect a particular context or geography and also allow us to work across institutions and geographical boundaries to advance sustainability worldwide?

A range of indicators can be used to compare the relative situations of countries, assess their strengths and weaknesses and identify domains where policy intervention is required. It would be much easier to have one list of indicators for everyone, allowing quick comparisons among different places and across time, but this is not so simple: what matters in California is not an exact match to what matters in Helsinki or Bangalore.

And yet, common indicators are needed if countries or localities want to compare their progress on sustainable development with others. From this, they can learn what works and what doesn't work. This is why, as measurement of sustainable development has evolved, many local, national and supra-national bodies such as the United Nations and the European Union have developed and refined sets of indicators. Along with international organisations and NGOs, they have put considerable effort into discussing and tuning their indicator sets to improve measurement of sustainable development and allow comparisons among countries or other levels of administration.

The Capital Approach

The key idea of sustainable development is the linkage between the well-being of the current generation and the well-being of future generations. To make this connection we can use the concept of capital. In economic terms, capital is a stock that is used in production over several years: think of a machine or a factory. Capital can be created by investment, and it is consumed over years and eventually wears out. The concept of capital can also be applied to sustainability, allowing us to measure all types of wealth that contribute to well-being more comprehensively. Economists use the concept of *national wealth* to indicate this broader measure.

The "Capital Approach" is a framework for measuring sustainable development which operates on the principle that sustaining well-being over time requires ensuring that we replace or conserve wealth in its different components. It emphasises the need to focus on the long-term determinants of development not to the exclusion of current needs, but rather according to a principle of sustainability: development that can be continued into the future. This approach allows us to discuss and evaluate how what we do now will work in the very near, medium and long-term, and how to talk about whether or not there is "progress", "regression" or "stagnation".

With this model, a society's total capital base encompasses five individual types:

> *financial capital* like stocks, bonds and currency deposits;

> *produced capital* like machinery, buildings, telecommunications and other types of infrastructure;

> *natural capital* in the form of natural resources, land and ecosystems providing services like waste absorption;

> *human capital* in the form of an educated and healthy workforce;

> *social capital* in the form of social networks and institutions.

Conceiving these different forms of capital as inputs into the production of well-being allows us to calculate national wealth as the sum of the different kinds of capital.

Sustainable development requires making sure that national wealth per capita does not decline over time and, when possible, that it increases. For example, if we consume all our natural capital and do nothing to preserve or increase it, this source of well-being will dry up, leading to unsustainable outcomes. The capital approach allows monitoring that capital stocks are not "drawn down" too low. Norway's management of its petroleum stocks provides a good example. With some of the world's largest petroleum reserves, Norway could spend the profits from the sale of its petroleum on any number of programmes. Instead, Norway invests these profits to be sure that when the oil reserves are depleted, other sources of income will be in place. To put it another way, just as financiers seek to maximise their capital base and the dividends it produces, we should maximise the financial, produced, human, social and natural capital base of our welfare and make sure it continues to pay dividends in terms of well-being over time.

This sounds very straightforward, but "maximising" capital involves making important decisions about what can be used up and what must be preserved. One important question: can the different types of capital be "substituted" for each other, as long as the total sum is maintained, or does each type have to be maintained at a certain minimum level? The practical answer to this question is that it depends on circumstances. In most circumstances, some specific categories of "critical capital" will be essential to the proper functioning of the world and our societies, things which perform essential functions and can be replaced at the margin only at huge costs.

A liveable climate is perhaps the most striking example it doesn't much matter what our national wealth adds up to, if climate change makes life on Earth or in certain parts of it impossible. Although environmental types of essential natural capital are the

Using technology to make architecture more sustainable

As we try to follow the model of sustainable development, among the first targets are the spaces in which we live and work. After all, what indicates human "development" more than the buildings and cities we construct? The 20th century saw several revolutions in architecture, with focuses ranging from aesthetic to productive to ecological. The role of technology has not been entirely positive, as the use of asbestos insulation shows.

In recent years, the movement towards more environmentally-friendly architecture, popularly called "Green Building", has grown significantly. In the US, this effort has been spearheaded by the Leadership in Energy and Environmental Design, or LEED, programme. LEED certifies new and renovated building projects on a scale up to "platinum", depending how many environmental "points" the project earns. Up to 70 points are awarded for aspects ranging from use of renewable energy and recycled materials to how close the site is to public transportation.

Experience now shows that prioritising the environment carries over to the social and economic pillars: the benefits of natural lighting on worker satisfaction and productivity are well-established; avoiding paints and glues with aggressive solvents improves worker health, thereby reducing sick days. Financially, the higher initial investment pays for itself in energy savings, increased leasing rates and longer building life.

In many European countries, stricter energy efficiency standards, in some cases accompanied by subsidies, are expanding the market for sustainable technologies. Such technologies then become mainstream among contractors and more affordable. Average electricity use per building is 30% lower in Germany than the US.

In the UK, a nation-wide initiative to make schools more sustainable is encouraging not just curriculum changes but innovative architecture. The most ambitious project to date is a primary school in Hertfordshire, where traditional environmental features like green roofs and rainwater re-use are accompanied by a state-of-the-art heat capture system under the playground that provides warm water in winter. In addition to the environmental benefits, students work and play in a healthier and more stimulating environment, carrying out experiments with insects from the sedum roof and studying the full life cycle of recycling with their own furniture.

The OECD Programme on Educational Building (PEB) promotes the exchange and analysis of policy, research and experience in all matters related to educational building. The PEB's goals are to improve the quality and suitability of educational buildings; ensure that the best use is made of the resources devoted to planning, building, running and maintaining educational buildings; and give early warning of the impact on educational building of trends in education and in society as a whole.

Source:
OECD Programme on Educational Building, *www.oecd.org/edu/facilities*.
Ouroussoff, N. (2007),
"Why are they greener than we are?",
New York Times Magazine, 20 May 2007,
www.nytimes.com.
Sustainable Schools,
www.teachernet.gov.uk/sustainableschools.
United States Green Building Council,
www.usgbc.org.
Walker, E. (2008), "Too cool for school:
Britain's most Eco-friendly building",
The Independent, 10 April 2008,
www.independent.co.uk/environment/green-living.

first to come to mind, aspects of social and human capital can also be critical. When the social networks and norms that are a basis for communities are depleted, societies break down, as in the case of conflict and war. Similarly, without education, human capital cannot be sustained, making overall sustainability impossible.

The global dimension

That said, many of the key issues for sustainable development are transboundary and even global, meaning they have impacts beyond political or geographical frontiers. Environmental issues such as air pollution or biodiversity loss are obvious examples, but economic and social questions are increasingly globalised too, trade or migration being the most obvious examples. Whatever measurement framework is used, it will need indicators to reflect sustainability for a variety of specific contexts and others that capture issues of global scale, such as climate change.

The WWF uses an analogy that is worth bearing in mind when trying to understand what indicators are and how they can be used. Think of a car. Dials and other displays give drivers a range of indicators as to how the car is performing, but not all of this information is relevant at any given time or for a given purpose. The oil temperature might be perfect, but if you run out of fuel the car is going to stop anyway. And bad drivers will still be a danger, no matter how many fancy gadgets are on the dashboard. Sustainability indicators are like the car's instruments, addressing individual items (energy reserves would be a direct analogy) or combining indicators across a number of domains to give a fuller picture (just as how "good" a car is depends on fuel consumption, safety, comfort, etc.).

Many companies have developed their own metrics for assessing the economic, environmental and social impacts of their facilities and products. Some are combining these into composites or simple indices, which are more likely to get the attention of CEOs. Larger corporations are also formulating ways to assess the sustainability of their supply chains of smaller companies. Ford of Europe, for instance, uses a Product Sustainability Index as a management tool to assess the potential impacts of motor vehicles on a range of factors. This is an engineering approach which combines eight indicators reflecting environmental (global warming potential,

Composite indicators

A composite indicator combines two or more individual indicators or "sub-indicators" into one number. Well-known examples include the Environmental Sustainability Index, the Ecological Footprint and the Human Development Index. Composites have the advantage of expressing complex information in a simple format, making it possible to rank factories, companies or countries in terms of their general sustainability. These simplified evaluations are very media-friendly and used somewhat like an academic grade.

From the point of view of statistical accuracy, though, composites have limitations. Composites may "compare apples and oranges", comparing things that are somehow essentially incomparable. The results or rankings depend on the way in which different indicators are weighted, leaving composites open to accusations of bias and lack of transparency.

Still, composites can give us a good idea of how a complex phenomenon, like "development" or "sustainable development", can be evaluated by looking at several important factors together. There are composites designed specifically to assess sustainability which include sub-indicators of each pillar. Other composites deal with one pillar in particular, but these are still often used in debates around sustainability. In the end, we can use composites for information function, their ability to provide an overview or summary of complex issues, and turn to other methods of measurement for more detailed analysis and decision-making.

materials use), social (mobility, capability, safety) and economic (lifecycle costs) vehicle attributes. Indicators are not aggregated into one ranking but rather tailored to the needs of various departments of the company.

Assessing sustainability

Indicators and sets of indicators are the basis for assessing progress on sustainability. Many different assessment methodologies exist, for example: regulatory impact assessments, poverty impact assessments, environmental impact assessments and strategic environmental assessments. But in these approaches, the exercise tends to focus on a particular pillar of sustainability and economic aspects tend to dominate. What we need are assessments that examine economic, environmental and social impacts and also the longer-term. In other words, we need sustainability impact assessments that can be applied to policies, programmes or agreements; to the national, regional or international levels; and to particular sectors of the economy.

Indicators and assessment tools already exist. The EU *Sustainability A-Test* site (*www.SustainabilityA-Test.net*) gives a good idea of the number of tools available. It presents 44 different types of tools for assessing sustainability classified into participatory processes, scenarios, multi-criteria analysis, cost-benefit analysis, accounting tools and models.

Whatever the methodology (indicators, models, surveys, cost-benefit analyses, cost-effectiveness studies), the procedures for conducting sustainability assessments have to be transparent and encourage the involvement of all concerned. The assessment has to be able to identify economic, environmental and social impacts but also the synergies and trade-offs across these dimensions. Different stages must be specified including a relevance test whether a sustainability assessment is even needed for the problem at hand.

Assessment results have to be presented to policy makers and others in clear and understandable terms. Even a well-designed assessment, carried out in a thorough manner, will have no influence if it neglects the political factors that impede its use. Most approaches may be too complex and too long for policy makers, while the existing bureaucracy may prefer traditional approaches rather than new assessment techniques. Moreover, sustainability assessments are often seen as an add-on rather than as an integral part of policy making. As a result, assessments may come too late with limited consideration of alternative policy options. Approaches for making better use of indicators and assessment tools are needed if we are to operationalise the concepts of sustainable development.

What constitutes the good life?

In essence, sustainable development is a means for improving our quality of life today in ways that can be maintained over time. It teaches us to value all that contributes to our well-being, even if like ecosystems their "worth" cannot be easily calculated. Our job as citizens, scientists or policy makers is to think through the best ways of including what is crucial to our existence in the balance sheet. And to make decisions that keep us out of the red.

Sustainable development has heavily influenced the debate on how we – societies and governments conceive of our role in the search for better, more balanced ways of living. In doing so, it has given new life to a conversation dating at least as far back as Plato: What constitutes the good life? And how does one go about creating it? These seemingly straightforward questions are not simple to answer. Happiness, satisfaction, well-being, welfare and wellness we use all of these concepts to express the idea of what gives life quality, of what makes it good. The questions that we pose as individuals are, in large part,those that drive the debate at the group level.

Thoroughly exploring what constitutes progress in these areas what the goals are, how far we are from reaching them, what kinds of trade-offs it will require to get there is the central task faced by citizens and governments. The tools and measures elaborated through sustainable development will continue to inform this exploration, providing a basis for the on-going work of improving the ways we govern and the ways we live.

Measurement of sustainable development helps us in two important tasks: evaluating where we are going and assessing the effects of specific policies, not only on the current generation, but also on future generations. One essential principle underlying any attempt at measurement is to understand what goes into the measurement process – what data are the most important, how they are collected, how they are compiled to provide evidence and how they can be expressed in different ways. For if we make ourselves smarter as an audience, then we can more easily select and understand the measurements we need to make good decisions, for us and for future generations.

Measuring progess in societies

Recent years have seen an explosion of interest around the world in the development of new, more comprehensive indicators of social progress. Despite the diversity of aims and approaches of these initiatives, they all seek to encourage positive social change. Yet, how can we ensure that this goal is reached? What sets of progress indicators are useful? And how are they used? We asked Kate Scrivens of the OECD's Global Project on Measuring the Progress of Societies to tell us.

What makes a successful set of progress indicators?
Successful outcomes can be defined in a number of ways. A policy change resulting from an indicator set being used in decision-making would be the most direct example. But you could also argue that media coverage of indicator data that raises public awareness is a success, too.

What is the aim of the OECD project?
Building sets of indicators requires a significant investment of time and resources. This can only be justified if you can reasonably expect there to be benefits from the exercise. Research into the circumstances under which indicator projects have been successful helps us to understand what works and what doesn't.

How are you going about it?
We're exploring the perspectives of a wide range of producers, users and advocates of progress indicators to spot common themes and best practices. We've adopted a 'before-during-after' approach, asking questions linked to distinct steps in the indicator development process.

The 'before' part examines how and why the indicator project came about. The aim here is to identify the issue that provided

the initial impetus and to assess that relevant data already existed.

'During' explores three separate aspects: project design and development; the final product; and communication and application.

The 'after' questions focus on outcomes. The idea is to evaluate how outcomes measure against the stated objectives, and to try to understand the main factors contributing to success or failure of the enterprise.

What kinds of project are you actually looking at?
We decided to pick examples that provided insight into a wide variety of situations. Among other things, that meant different levels of geographic coverage, so we looked for multinational, national and sub-national projects. In line with the 'Measuring Progress' philosophy, the research focuses on indicator sets designed to give a comprehensive view of society, rather than being issue-specific.

Are any of the projects about sustainable development?
Yes, we'll look at the EU sustainable development indicators and structural indicators underpinning the Lisbon agenda for growth and innovation as examples of multinational indicators. It's generally felt that the Lisbon indicators were driven mainly by political considerations, while the sustainable development indicators were shaped by more technical expertise. It will be interesting to compare the two, and to see how indicators are developed in a regional forum, such as the EU.

To find out more, visit
www.oecd.org/progress.

Find Out More

... FROM OECD

On the Internet

For a general introduction to OECD work on sustainable development, visit *www.oecd.org/sustainabledevelopment.*

Publications

Conducting Sustainability Assessments (2008):
This volume reviews the state of the art in assessing sustainability. It covers methodologies and tools and current practice in OECD countries, as well as the debate on quantifying and comparing diverse types of short- and long-term policy impacts.

OECD Factbook 2008: Economic, Environmental and Social Statistics
OECD Factbook 2008 presents over 100 indicators covering the economy, agriculture, education, energy, the environment, foreign aid, health and quality of life, industry, information and communications, population/labour force, trade and investment, taxation, public expenditure and R&D.

Statistics, Knowledge and Policy 2007: Measuring and Fostering the Progress of Societies
Is life getting better? Are our societies making progress? Indeed, what does "progress" mean to the world's citizens? The OECD's 2nd World Forum on Statistics, Knowledge and Policy 'Measuring and Fostering the Progress of Societies' brought together a diverse group of leaders from more than 130 countries to debate these issues.

Statistics, Knowledge and Policy: Key Indicators to Inform Decision Making (2006):
This publication discusses why indicator systems are useful and how statistics can be used, how to implement systems related to different kinds of statistics, and what systems are already in place.

Handbook on Constructing Composite Indicators: Methodology and User Guide (2008):
This Handbook is a guide for constructing and using composite indicators that compare and rank country performance in areas such as industrial competitiveness, sustainable development, globalisation and innovation.

Measuring Sustainable Development: Integrated Economic, Environmental and Social Frameworks (2004):
The papers contained in this volume address the various conceptual, measurement and statistical policy issues that arise when applying accounting frameworks to this complex problem.

Also of interest

UNECE/OECD/Eurostat Working Group on Statistics for Sustainable Development, **Report on Measuring Sustainable Development** (forthcoming 2008):
This report presents the capital framework for selecting indicators for measuring sustainable development.
www.oecd.org/sustainabledevelopment

Alternative Measures of Well-Being, an OECD Social, Employment and Migration Working Paper (2006):
This report assesses whether GDP per capita is an adequate proxy as a measure of well-being or whether other indicators used either as substitutes or as complements to GDP per capita are more suitable.
http://dx.doi.org/10.1787/71322233 2167.

7

How do societies change or evolve? Whether the means to solve problems on a global scale come through technological innovation, changing consumption patterns or providing access to important services, progress depends on the complex interactions of people, businesses, NGOs and government. Learning to co-ordinate these is key to making real gains in sustainable development.

Government
and Civil Society

By way of introduction...

In February 2008, rioters in Burkina-Faso took to the streets, angry at the jump in food and fuel prices over the past year. They burned petrol stations, trashed government buildings and stoned a government delegation that had come to discuss the problem. Within a few weeks, similar scenes were repeated in over 30 countries around the world, from Haiti to Somalia, Yemen to Indonesia. The world's poorest were not the only ones feeling the pinch. Italians and Mexicans were also up in arms over the cost of pasta and tortillas, whose price has considerable symbolic value. In the year leading up to the crisis, prices for many staple foods, including wheat and rice, doubled or even quadrupled. The consequences were visible to consumers on shop shelves worldwide, and the effects ranged from the plummeting popularity of governments to the riots described above.

The food crisis illustrates many of the themes we've talked about throughout this book and emphasises the need for a co-ordinated and coherent approach to sustainable development. The interaction of economic, social and environmental factors produced the crisis. What are these factors? As the world economy has expanded, prices of all commodities have increased. Higher standards of living have driven up demand for beef and dairy products, and added to the energy needs of modern agriculture, already a big consumer of oil and other petroleum products for pesticides, fertilisers and transport. Planting crops for biofuel intended to reduce dependency on oil has taken land away from food production, tightening supply and driving prices higher. Major food producers, including Australia and Myanmar, have been hit by droughts and cyclones respectively, further limiting supply. Changes in international trade have led some countries to rely on imports, whose prices they can no longer afford.

▶ Given the number of factors involved, can anybody control what is happening? Is it possible to reconcile so many conflicting interests? Do we have the means to guide agriculture and other vital activities towards new ways of doing things? This chapter argues that changes, whether negative or positive, do not simply "happen". It looks at how governments and civil society can set local, national and global communities on the path of sustainable development.

Making changes

At its most basic, politics is about making decisions on what is important to a society and how these important issues should be handled. It is a process by which people and groups who may not agree attempt to translate their beliefs into workable rules, or laws, to regulate life within a community. The structures of government that manage these processes are often conservative and the impetus for new thinking has often come from outside. In many cases of major societal change, the pressure to transform laws and attitudes has come from visionary individuals and groups, or "civil society organisations" arguing their case until a critical mass of public opinion and political backing has been reached. Then, what was new and at times shocking, irritating or seemingly impossible, became the norm a part of our political and social fabric.

Think of the changes developed countries have seen over the past 100 years. At the start of the 20th century, horses and walking were the main means of transport, even in the rich metropolises like Berlin, London or New York. If a street was lit at all, it was probably by gaslight. Before penicillin, infectious diseases were often fatal. Women were killed in the fight for the right to vote. Go back a few decades more and slavery was considered normal. Children under 10 years old worked 12-hour shifts in factories, as they still do in some countries today.

How did conditions and attitudes change? How was what seemed natural and unchangeable swept away? There's no single cause for the major changes in human history. Visionary individuals argued and organised for change. Sometimes a book or other cultural event provoked a shift in conventional thinking – Dickens' *Oliver Twist* cast a harsh light on England's 1834 Poor Law Amendment, while Upton Sinclair's novel *The Jungle*, published in 1906, showed the appalling working and sanitary conditions in the meat industry contributing directly to the creation of the US Food and Drug Administration.

What can this teach us about improving the world? About increasing well-being for people today, as well as leaving a world fit for future generations to make the changes they will deem necessary? Whether solutions come through introducing new technologies, changing consumption patterns or providing access to health care, water and sanitation, the fact is that any and all improvements depend on the co-operation of a number of different actors who interact in a complex and dynamic way.

Moving from a traditional development model to one of sustainable development has been, and will continue to be, a transformation along these same lines. Whereas in the past most development decisions were driven primarily by economic considerations without regard to implications for the social or environmental spheres, the last 20 or so years of discussions around sustainability have transformed the way both public and private institutions conceive of growth, quality of life and other development-related concerns.

Citizens, civil society and progress

Just as no inventor alone in the garage has the means to turn a discovery into a meaningful tool for society, no activist can alone achieve widespread social change. Each of them must communicate and interact with others to prove the merits of the new discovery or idea and convince others to adopt and promote it. Human advancement depends on an ongoing exchange between people and institutions. The decisions we make about how the world should be and how it can be improved depend on interactions among individual citizens, businesses, civil society and governments. These four categories function together in the complex and sometimes chaotic process of decision-making that we call politics.

The term civil society is one we hear a great deal today, one which like sustainable development can be hard to pin down to an exact definition on which everyone agrees. The London School of Economics Centre for Civil Society defines it as "the arena of uncoerced collective action around shared interests, purposes and values.

The groups, associations and movements that make up civil society have played a part in all the important societal changes in the past century or more. Civil society organisations can be dedicated to specific issues or more general struggles. Indeed, they have been key to the success of very significant advances including universal suffrage, environmental protection, workers' rights and combating racial discrimination.

Sustainable development is no exception. Organisations such as the Sierra Club, founded in 1892 in the US, or Australia's Gould Group, dating from 1909, were advocating what we would now term sustainability long before politicians and the media gave the matter much thought. Civil society organisations have been present at all

Downwinders at Risk

Becky Bornhorst considers herself lucky – mother, homemaker, she loves her neighbourhood, her city, her lifestyle. But when she looks at the smoke pluming in the distance – an all too familiar fixture in the horizon – she feels frustrated. Becky knows that the cement kilns a few miles away emit levels of mercury considered dangerous to human health. For over ten years she has contributed to efforts to regulate effects of this and other forms of pollution through a very active local NGO, part of a network of groups trying to improve environmental quality in the North Texas region.

"I was a stay-at-home Mom in 1987 when I began hearing stories about hazardous waste burning at the three cement plants down the road in Midlothian, Texas" recounts Becky. "My son was four and my daughter just one year old. I found a notice in our local newspaper about an early childhood parent-teacher meeting with speakers discussing the cement plants."

Becky went to the meeting with a couple of other mothers and immediately joined other concerned citizens to form Downwinders at Risk. "My goal was to protect my children – I didn't think we should have to run away from the pollution. But I was naïve. I thought we'd clean up the air easily just by organising. It has proved not to be so easy."

Becky and her colleagues have participated in hundreds of formal hearings and discussions with local and national authorities. They have made progress along the way, winning some important improvements in their efforts to curb the emissions and clean up the air, with support from across the political spectrum.

Yet the rapid growth that has occurred in her area has meant that overall reductions in pollution have not yet been achieved. "My kids are now in college and I'm still trying to clean the air," she states matter-of-factly. "I never cease to be amazed at the political power of industry and citizen's lack of it."

The need to balance industrial activities considered important to a local economy against the potential health risks of pollution and citizen's quality of life is a challenge facing virtually every community. And it has very often been the case that a problem of environmental degradation has to reach a critical point – for example, at which air quality reaches a dangerous enough level to cause health threats, forcing people to stay inside their homes – before any action is taken to prevent or mitigate the polluting processes.

How important is air quality? What are the health consequences of pollution? The costs? When is it too late to take action to reverse a dangerous trend? These questions are among the thorniest facing societies today. The level of growth in human activity due to industrialisation has produced what could be seen as a turning point in the late 20th century – the point at which the negative consequences of environmental loss and destruction became starkly evident and at which, simultaneously, standards of living in the developed world reached a level such that meeting basic needs was no longer the central task of most people. In other words, focus began to shift from meeting basic needs to also reflecting on the consequences of human activity. From development alone to sustainable development.

of the major meetings that put sustainable development on the map. In fact, they have been instrumental in developing sustainability as an idea and in its translation into concrete practices. They have consultative status at UN and OECD meetings (inclusion that they had to organise and work for) and participate in policy debates. They do research, write policy briefs, and organise collective social action like protests and boycotts. They raise awareness and help educate the public and policy makers.

We talked about the food crisis at the start of this chapter. The Marine Stewardship Council (MSC) is a concrete example of what a civil society organisation can achieve in a domain like this. The MSC is an independent, global, non-profit organisation set up to find a solution to the problem of overfishing. It was first established by Unilever, the world's largest buyer of seafood, and WWF in 1997. In 1999, it became fully independent from both organisations. The MSC works with fisheries, retailers and others to identify, certify, and promote responsible, environmentally appropriate, socially beneficial and economically viable fishing practices around the world.

The MSC Principles and Criteria for Sustainable Fishing is an internationally recognised set of principles to assess whether a fishery is well managed and sustainable. Only products from fisheries assessed by independent certifiers as meeting the standard are able to use the MSC logo on their products. For the first time, this gives consumers a way to identify – and the choice to purchase – fish and other seafood from well-managed sources.

What is the role of government?

A 2003 poll of Canadians showed that car salespeople are trusted less than almost any other profession, with only 10% of respondents finding them trustworthy. *Almost* any other: "national politicians" do even worse, at only 9%. Other people show similar opinions to the Canadians. Government itself is often criticised for a long list of failures, real or perceived: stifling innovation and entrepreneurship through taxes and red tape, caving in to pressure from lobbies and non-representative interest groups, leaving education or health care systems in poor condition. Governing in such a complex world is a huge challenge. Yet democratic governments at least try to make policies that will satisfy people and take care of important issues.

Before looking in more detail at the various tools governments can use, it's useful to recall what tasks governments perform in working for sustainable development. In general, through their data gathering and analysis, policy making and co-ordination, governments can provide support and leadership for moving society in a given direction. They can make sure that individual interests do not detract from the common good. Sustainable development contributes to this good, but actions to promote it may negatively affect the immediate interests of certain people, such as the shareholders of a factory that has to pay higher wages or install air and water filters.

Governments also intervene to deal with what economists call "market failures", situations in which market forces alone do not produce the most efficient outcome. The "externalities" mentioned in Chapter 5 on production and consumption would be an example of this – situations where the actions of one individual or group have costly consequences for others.

Given the global nature of many of the challenges facing sustainability, nations have to co-operate at the highest levels to design and apply solutions. National governments have the authority and power to do this. They also have the means to ensure that decisions are applied. The three most important means by which governments can influence sustainable development (for better or worse) are regulation, taxation and spending. Each can play a role, but taxes tend to be more cost-effective and flexible than regulations, while subsidies are expensive for taxpayers and consumers.

Regulation

As we said earlier, governments may introduce new regulations in response to social or other pressures, but regulation can in turn have a marked effect on behaviour. Smoking in public places would probably continue without government intervention to ban it, for example. Good regulation is an essential tool for making sustainable development a reality. Social and economic conditions evolve, new materials and technologies are developed, and our understanding of health and environmental effects improves. We have to adapt regulations to correspond to changing conditions, and there will always be a need for new regulation. Nanotechnologies and biotechnologies hold great promise, but they also raise a number of questions regarding their safety and in some cases the ethical implications of their adoption. Governments have to gather and analyse the evidence and see if there is a need to change or create regulation. Their decisions will have a major impact on how these technologies and the industries that use them develop.

Nanotech and biotech reveal one of the weaknesses of regulation – the pace of change in some areas is far faster than the pace at which the regulator works. In other cases, governments may try to move more quickly than the electorate is prepared for – many people are hostile to changes in legislation that affect their working conditions or pensions for instance. Regulation has other limits, too. If, for example, bans were 100% effective, there would be no illegal drug use, no speeding, in fact no crime or delinquency to worry about at all. Moreover, the way bans, restrictions, standards and other types of regulation are drafted and applied can also cause problems, leading to counterproductive "red tape". Instead of providing a coherent framework for activity, red tape hinders innovation, stifles initiative and adds unnecessary administrative burdens to economic and social activity.

Regulation can however lead to desirable outcomes for sustainability and increase individual well-being and that of society as a whole. Vaccination and other public health initiatives are good examples, as is the obligation to educate children. We take some of these regulations so much for granted that we may be surprised to learn that they are comparatively recent and had to be fought for, such as regulations concerning the quality of drinking water and food or the safety and environmental impact of automobiles.

Regulation then is not inherently good or bad. This point is recognised in a set of guiding principles for regulatory quality and performance established by the OECD. The importance attached to identifying how any proposed changes to regulation might affect other policy objectives is especially important for sustainable development, where changes in one area may have important consequences elsewhere. The principles also stress that regulation affects, and is affected, by other types of intervention, notably government spending and subsidies and taxes. These are discussed below.

Spending

Governments are big spenders and the way they allocate funds influences practically every aspect of the economy and society. This can have direct impacts on sustainability. A government with a certain sum to devote to transport can decide to invest it in improving the road network or in developing rail services. It can use the energy budget to build new electricity generating capacity or to promote insulation and other energy-saving technologies. Health spending can focus on developing innovative therapies or on preventing common pathologies. International aid can be used to encourage bilateral trade or to promote technical co-operation. In everything from science budgets to welfare programmes, the choices governments make have an impact.

This section focuses on a type of spending the public is generally less familiar with, but which makes up a significant part of most national budgets: subsidies. Many OECD governments subsidise fossil energy, and removing or reforming these subsidies would help policies to tackle climate change. Agriculture may seem a less obvious example, but it is one of the main beneficiaries of subsidies. Consumers and taxpayers transfer over $300 billion to OECD agriculture each year. Some of this is used to help improve agricultural techniques or quality, but much of it keeps prices high. For example, despite reforms, average OECD domestic prices for rice, sugar and milk are still more than double those on world markets, which is particularly hard on poorer consumers who spend proportionately more than the rich on food.

> "Subsidies often introduce economic, environmental and social distortions with unintended consequences. They are expensive for governments and may not achieve their objectives while also inducing harmful environmental and social outcomes."
>
> *Subsidy Reform and Sustainable Development:*
> *Political Economy Aspects*

Historically, the goal of farm subsidies has been to increase production and therefore food security for a given nation. Over the course of the 20th century, this has meant increasingly mechanised agriculture, a shift towards single crop (monocrop) cultivation, heavy reliance on fertilisers and pesticides, and depending on climate, drainage and irrigation schemes. This so-called "high input" agriculture resulted in a boom in production. At the start of the 20th century, an American farmer had to feed on average 2.5 people in the country. Today, a farmer feeds over 130 people according to the National Academy of Engineering, and estimates that include exports are even higher.

These advances have major impacts on the environment and on farming communities:

➤ Highly mechanised agriculture can result in increased soil erosion, as machines break up the soil. This results not only in a loss of fertility locally, but also in water pollution as these sediments run off the surface.

➤ Conversion from small, diverse fields with hedges to monocrop reduces the niches available to insects and birds. European farmland bird populations have declined by 40% in the last 30 years, and for all but a few species that trend is continuing.

➤ Nutrient pollution (eutrophication) is the leading water pollution issue. In most areas, farms are the largest source of the nitrogen and phosphorus at the root of these harmful algal blooms.

➤ Previously pure sources of groundwater are now contaminated by pesticides that have leached through the soil from farms above.

➤ Irrigation is the largest human use of freshwater, accounting for over 70% of the total worldwide. Reduced river flow and dropping groundwater levels make this use a potential source of conflict. In the case of rivers and other surface waters, habitat for fish and birds is sacrificed to maintain food production.

"Decoupling" aid from production is a key measure: goals for agriculture are changing, and subsidies can be a powerful tool for reaching those new goals. Once again, the food crisis illustrates how numerous strands are interwoven. High prices weaken the case for subsidies and could enable funds to be freed for other uses. But high prices also encourage farmers to produce more. They may as a result abandon schemes to leave land uncultivated so that it can be used for other purposes, such as to encourage biodiversity. Carefully targeted subsidies can help to restore the balance among various policy objectives: this requires transparency regarding who benefits and who pays for subsidies such as the European Union's Common Agricultural Policy (CAP), and careful co-ordination between the many stakeholders.

"Subsidy reform...can lead to fiscal savings, structural adjustment and enhanced efficiency and productivity in production. Environmentally, the reduction of harmful subsidies can lower negative externalities such as pollution and waste. Socially, subsidy reform can lead to a more equitable distribution of income and balanced long-run growth of communities and countries."

Subsidy Reform and Sustainable Development:
Economic, Environmental and Social Aspects

The impacts of agricultural subsidies (positive or negative) obviously touch the social sphere as well as the economy and the environment. Indeed, it is hoped that the reform of agricultural subsidies will allow farmers from developing countries to compete in the global market. This potential for profit should encourage the development of farming infrastructure in countries that have not traditionally exported, with important implications for local employment, purchasing power and food supply. As seen in the opening of this chapter, food security is once again a concern – worldwide – and all governments will have to develop appropriate measures for encouraging productive and sustainable agriculture.

Taxation and emissions trading

The flip side of the spending coin is, of course, taxes. When we think of taxes and sustainability, so-called "green" or "ecotaxes" come to mind first, since these (like emissions trading) are designed to contribute directly to environmental sustainability by making "bad" environmental behaviours more costly. However, as we've argued throughout, the environment is only one part of the process. The social and economic aspects of sustainability are influenced by taxes, too, and in fact are among the biggest items in national budgets. Education for example represents 5% of government spending in OECD countries on average, while health accounts for another 6%. But since "social taxes" existed long before the concept of sustainable development was invented, and their role is rarely presented in this light, their importance is easy to overlook. Nonetheless, through mechanisms such as social welfare schemes, they play an essential role in addressing issues that market mechanisms and private initiatives alone cannot deal with efficiently.

> **"The environmental effectiveness and economic efficiency of environmentally related taxes could be improved further if existing exemptions and other special provisions were scaled back, and if the tax rates were better aligned with the magnitude of the negative environmental impacts to be addressed."**
>
> *The Political Economy of Environmentally Related Taxes*

Likewise, taxes are often perceived as hindering economic development, but governments use them and the revenues derived from them to shape and promote economic development. The social and economic roles of taxation overlap in many cases too, as when funds are invested in developing certain sectors or regions, or when social measures are used to ease or encourage the transition from traditional to new activities.

Interestingly, for many sustainable development issues there is a very strong argument to be made in favour of using taxation and other market-based mechanisms *instead* of subsidies: what are the chances that policy makers will identify every initiative worthy of support and make the appropriate subsidy, without accidentally supporting some initiatives which turn out to have negative effects? On the other hand, a very simple taxation mechanism can spur innovation on the part of businesses, as they come up with their own solutions to reduce a particular practice.

There are several reasons to use economic tools for sustainable development:

➤ They can provide incentives for behaviour that fits with sustainable development goals and deter actions that go against those goals.

➤ Overall environmental, social and economic costs could be built into prices using such measures, driving markets towards a more sustainable economy.

➤ They encourage innovation by providing market pressure.

➤ The revenue generated could be used to reduce other taxes or finance social measures.

A May 2008 Chicago Tribune article put it like this: "They [consumers] can pay high prices to oil producers or to themselves. The tax proceeds can be used to finance programs of value here at home or to pay for cuts in other taxes even as they curb the release of carbon dioxide."

National strategies: putting sustainable development to work in governments

The governments that signed Agenda 21 at the Rio Earth Summit expressed a certain degree of optimism about sustainable development. For them, the role of government would be central in achieving those goals. It makes sense: sustainable development is a concept with the potential to change many things for the better, but if not firmly anchored in policy-making bodies at all levels of government local, regional, national and international concrete achievements will remain elusive.

In the same way, if policies within one government ministry undermine those in another, progress stalls. Before promoting large-scale tourism for example, it may be wise to ask if the golf courses and swimming pools will mean there's no water left for farmers. On the other hand, if you favour agriculture over tourism, you may lose the chance to create hundreds of jobs in an area with high unemployment. Governing for sustainable development doesn't mean favouring one aspect and neglecting the others; it's about finding the most coherent balance among different claims and devising the most efficient administrative and other means to implement strategies.

> **"While many countries have formulated and implemented national strategies for sustainable development, many lack the basic design and implementation elements recommended by both the OECD and the UN."**
>
> *Institutionalising Sustainable Development*

But how do you go about making plans for what you would like to accomplish? Agenda 21 signatories agreed to develop National Sustainable Development Strategies (NSDS), documents intended to fit the specific needs and goals of different countries while addressing the basic sustainable development priorities that the international community (OECD and UN) has agreed on. Given the flexibility allowed, strategies vary widely. Most OECD countries now have an NSDS in place, each with particular strengths and weaknesses. So over fifteen years on from Rio, how are they doing? Are certain countries or regions leading the way? If so, how do they do it?

A recent OECD workshop on best practices for institutionalising sustainable development gave some concrete suggestions. Participants identified a number of indicators of success such as inscribing sustainable development in constitutions and legislation and including it in national budgeting processes. In the following section we'll describe how governments are trying to meet the goals of their national strategies in practice.

What works?

An essential part of a programme's success is its perceived importance. For sustainable development to be taken seriously, it needs to be centrally located in a ministry or department with influence across all government activities in the Prime Ministry as in the case of Austria or in the Ministry of Finance as in Norway. When sustainable development is "anchored" in one of these central functions, its impact is enhanced and more easily co-ordinated throughout the different parts of government. Sustainable development can also have its own ministry as in the case of France.

> "Institutionalising sustainable development, whether through national strategies or other means, will not happen if the person at the top is not determined to make it happen."
> Jim MacNeil, Secretary General of the World Commission on Environment and Development in *Institutionalising Sustainable Development*

In the case of new sustainable development ministries, a diverse range of concerns previously separated across government ministries are re-grouped into one. Putting energy, ecology, maritime affairs, territorial planning, forestry and other domains together allows for integrated analysis and decision-making and makes it easier to avoid the pitfall of policies that contradict and undermine each other. Yet this approach can only be effective if supported by the prime minister or presiden in other words, if its recommendations translate into concrete implementations.

New Zealand shows how the social dimension can be included. The Sustainable Development in New Zealand programme gives equal weight to social sustainable development in relation to the economy and environment, with special attention to demographic trends, new roles of women in society, improvements in health and housing, and better integration of Maori communities.

What does governance for sustainability look like?

> **"Liveable cities with high-quality infrastructure, green spaces, and inner city residential areas and public projects can contribute to economic success, attracting foreign investors as well as highly qualified professionals and tourists."**
>
> *Competitive Cities in the Global Economy*

It sounds great in theory, but in practice? The Vauban neighbourhood of Freiburg in Germany was founded on the principles of sutainable living. The idea was to use intelligent planning and design to co-ordinate the different areas of daily life: traffic, building, energy, sanitation, public space and nature. Colourful three-storey structures are interspersed with gardens and playgrounds. Children attend the on-site pre-school and primary. Stores are within walking distance of homes.

For children and adolescents, unicycles seem to be the favorite means of transport. You won't see lots of cars – nearly half of the residents have agreed to go car-free. Speed limits are only 5km per hour, making the streets safe for pedestrians and cyclists.

With a tram line and several bus stops, Vauban is easily accessible by public transport. Freiburg is also home to one of the first "carshare" programmes, where residents pay a small charge to use a car or van when they need one. Construction for this "sustainable model district" respects a low energy consumption standard, where all of the houses beat standard new constructions in energy efficiency, and an additional 150 "plus energy" units produce more energy than they use.

Vauban also gave homebuyers the chance to take a greater role in designing their living space through the co-operative system. It allowed individual residents to invest in a new set of units together and work as a group to decide on customising their building. Not only does this add a creative element to housing, it gives a different meaning to the notion of investment – of the buyer's time, effort and ideas.

Vauban hasn't solved all the problems, but it seems to be doing better than many more ambitious projects, and its experience provides concrete examples of success. As far as governance is concerned, it shows the importance of the "micro" level – listening to the people who are actually going to live in a street before planning that street. It also shows the importance of coherence among the different layers of government. Social diversity objectives were hit by cuts to subsidised housing. Balancing different social interests can be hard, too. The need to spend more public money on children is provoking intergenerational tensions.

But no scheme is perfect, and governance is also about tackling difficulties. Vauban and Freibourg are now cited around the world as examples of sustainable living. The project shows that when governments and citizens get together to apply the principles of sustainability life is more pleasant. And the kids whizzing around on their unicycles would probably tell you it's more fun.

Intergenerational questions are an important component of the social dimension, which is why the *Swedish Strategy for Sustainable Development* adopted an intergenerational timeframe which includes a vision for the future which should remain valid for a generation or at least 25 years.

Sustainability in all levels of government

Leadership at the national level is one key part of governance for sustainable development. However, initiatives at regional and local levels are also critical to its success. After all, local governments have the closest proximity to what people and businesses actually do how they pollute, how they produce and consume, how they experience health care and education systems. People usually decide to take action on a given issue because of what they perceive in their immediate environment and local governments have a lot to do with how a place looks, feels and functions.

Local governments have to identify the critical relations among many factors likely to shape economic, social, political and environmental quality. But even the city level administration may be too remote from the day to day impacts of decisions. Effective governance also needs lower level local networks that include non-governmental actors, associations and businesses, for example to deal with social tensions or make the most of economic opportunities. As the UK Commission for Sustainable Development says: "National policy sets direction, but it's practical action at the local level that makes sustainable development real."

Identifying the correct level of government for addressing a question is itself an important and often complex task. Large cities or metropolitan regions, for example, regroup a number of localities with divergent views on issues important to the greater metro area, as well as different ways of dealing with the range of problems cities handle. Also, many sustainability issues are "regional" in nature think of air pollution or land use. Coherent governance for sustainable development for these large urban areas often requires a regional institution that can co-ordinate efforts and solve inconsistencies in local policies and initiatives.

Furthermore, strategies that are seen as simply one more government programme imposed from above have less chance of succeeding than those defined through consultation and debate.

The rise of biofuels – a cautionary tale

In the 1920s Henry Ford designed the Model T to run on an ethanol blend, and even constructed a corn fermentation plant in Kansas, but the discovery of oil in Texas and elsewhere made petrol the dominant transport fuel. Corn-to-ethanol saw a resurgence in the US following the oil shocks, and Brazil invested heavily in ethanol from sugar cane, making it a major fuel in that market. At the close of the 20th century, amid concern about climate change, ethanol's advocates argued that in theory, ethanol could provide carbon-neutral fuel; petrol with 15% ethanol would not require any changes to vehicle design or driver lifestyle. Although ethanol does release CO_2 during combustion, the feed plants also absorb CO_2 as they grow. Basically, next year's ethanol crop would clean up this year's carbon emissions. Other advantages include providing farm income and energy security for countries that can devote agricultural land to these crops. Similarly, vegetable oils derived from plants ranging from rapeseed to oil palm can be used in diesel engines.

Sound perfect? Western governments jumped on the bandwagon, with a 2003 EU directive mandating 5.75% biofuel content in transportation fuels by 2010. Worldwide, ethanol production doubled and biodiesel quadrupled in 2000-05.

But clouds are gathering. Environmentalists have been warning for years that dependence on biofuels will not only exacerbate the negative impact of conventional monocrop agriculture (habitat loss, freshwater use and run-off of fertilizers and pesticides), but may not even be carbon neutral at all. For certain ethanol crops, energy used for tractors, fertilizer production and fermentation processes may end up producing more CO_2 than the crops absorb. The sharpest environmental debate has come as vast tracts of Indonesian peatland rainforest have been burned and replaced with oil palm – representing up to 10% of global carbon emissions over the past few years, and a doubling in the rate of habitat loss for unique species such as orang-utans.

In the social sphere, Mexico City's so-called "Tortilla Riots" in February 2007 were linked to price rises following increased demand for corn from the US ethanol industry. Spring 2008 saw commodity price increases and food shortages that drive home the absurdity of turning food crops into fuel. So are we nearing the end of the road for biofuels? The great hope remains that we will develop efficient technologies for generating ethanol or biodiesel from crop residues, "weed" plants or algae. This may involve genetically engineering new microbes to ferment cellulose into ethanol. In the meantime, the EU is reconsidering the 2003 directive as we learn more about biofuel's wide-ranging impacts.

Source:

BBC News (2007), "Quick Guide: Biofuels", BBC News, 25 Jan 2007, *http://news.bbc.co.uk.*

Harrabin, R. (2008), "EU rethinks biofuels guidelines", BBC News, 14 Jan 2008, *http://news.bbc.co.uk.*

OECD (2008), *An Economic Assessment of Biofuel Environmental Policies,* *www.oecd.org/tad/bioenergy.*

Rosenthal, E. (2008), "Once a Dream Fuel, Palm Oil May Be an Eco-Nightmare", *The New York Times*, 31 Jan 2008, *www.nytimes.com.*

It would be unrealistic to imagine that everybody would be satisfied with every aspect of a national strategy, but the strategy is more likely to be implemented if everyone concerned has a chance to influence outcomes. This is why the Czech Government Council for Sustainable Development includes government, business, academics, NGOs and other stakeholders and serves as the umbrella group for developing, implementing and revising the national sustainable development strategy.

Many countries seem to be making progress towards governance for sustainable development. Yet the development of NSDS, no matter how complete, by no means guarantees that goals will be reached that depends in each case how strategies are translated into laws and regulations and how the different levels of government (national, regional and local) manage to execute them.

The governance of uncertainty

The media often emphasise the role of corporations and individuals in sustainable development – after all we're the ones building, purchasing, and so on – but governments play an equally significant role and can have far more influence than even the biggest multinational. Their ability to influence behaviours and co-ordinate efforts can make all the difference in producing substantial results. If not coherent, though, government actions can be a barrier to improvement.

When describing the role of government, it's easy to give the impression that governance for sustainable development is merely a matter of identifying objectives then putting in place a series of measures and bodies to oversee them. It's not. Just about every aspect of the economy, society, and the physical resources on which they ultimately depend, influences sustainability. Outcomes depend on an infinite number of interactions working on different timescales of varying importance. No model, however robust, no foresight, however penetrating, can tell us everything we'd like to know. Governments attempting to implement sustainability have to deal with this uncertainty. Not only their goals, but the strategies and instruments used to achieve them must be sustainable, too. They must be rigorous enough to be effective, but flexible enough to adapt as circumstances and priorities evolve. In the face of uncertainty, governance itself has to be sustainable.

Find Out More

On the Internet

For a general introduction to OECD work on sustainable development or governance, visit *www.oecd.org/sustainabledevelopment* and *www.oecd.org/governance*.

Publications

Institutionalising Sustainable Development (2007):
"Institutionalisation" embeds the concept of sustainable development in government operations for the long-term and reduces the vulnerability of sustainable development aims to shorter-term political objectives. This volume contains recommendations for true institutionalisation.

Subsidy Reform and Sustainable Development: Political Economy Aspects (2007):
Eliminating unsustainable subsidies requires comprehensive approaches that are supported by top political leadership, transparent in their potential effects on all parties, consistent over the long term, and often accompanied by transition supports. This volume uses sectoral case studies to illustrate that achieving change in structural policies depends largely on good governance.

Subsidy Reform and Sustainable Development: Economic, Environmental and Social Aspects (2006):
This report reviews approaches for assessing subsidies and associated taxes, and looks at country experiences in reforming subsidies in the agriculture, fisheries, industry, and transport sectors.

Environmental Performance of Agriculture at a Glance (2008):
This report provides the latest and most comprehensive data and analysis on the environmental performance of agriculture in OECD countries since 1990. It covers key environmental themes including soil, water, air and biodiversity and looks at recent policy developments in all 30 countries.

Power to the People? Building Open and Inclusive Policy Making (forthcoming 2008):
This book charts emerging practice in ensuring policy-making processes are more open and inclusive and gathers an impressive array of diverse opinions from leading practitioners. It offers a set of guiding principles to support open and inclusive policy making and service delivery in practice.

Environmentally Harmful Subsidies: Challenges for Reform (2005):
Subsidies are pervasive throughout OECD countries and much of this support is potentially harmful environmentally. This report presents sectoral analyses on agriculture, fisheries, water, energy and transport, proposing a checklist approach to identifying and assessing environmentally harmful subsidies. It also identifies the key tensions and conflicts that are likely to influence subsidy policy making.

Also of interest

An OECD Framework for Effective and Efficient Environmental Policies (2008):
www.oecd.org/envmin2008

Good Practices in the National Sustainable Development Strategies of OECD Countries (2006):
www.oecd.org/sustainabledevelopment

Agriculture and the Environment: Lessons Learned from a Decade of OECD Work (2004):
www.oecd.org/tad/env

References

Chapter 1

Diamond, J. (2005), *Collapse: How Societies Choose to Fail Or Succeed*, Penguin, New York.

Maddison, A. (2001), *The World Economy: A Millenial Perspective*, OECD Publishing, Paris.

OECD (2003), *Emerging Risks in the 21st Century: An Agenda for Action*, OECD Publishing, Paris.

OECD (2005), "Preserving Biodiversity and Promoting Biosafety", *OECD Policy Briefs*, OECD Publishing, Paris.

OECD (2007), "2007 Annual Report on Sustainable Development Work in the OECD", *www.oecd.org/dataoecd/38/21/40015309.pdf*.

OECD (2007), *Institutionalising Sustainable Development*, OECD Sustainable Development Studies, OECD Publishing, Paris.

UNDP (2007), *Human Development Report 2007/2008: Fighting Climate Change: Human Solidarity in a divided world*, Palgrave Macmillan, New York.

Chapter 2

OECD (2001), *Sustainable Development: Critical Issues*, OECD Publishing, Paris.

OECD (2006), "Advancing Sustainable Development", *OECD Policy Briefs*, OECD Publishing, Paris.

OECD (2007), "OECD Contribution to the United Nations Commission on Sustainable Development 15: Energy for Sustainable Development", *www.oecd.org/dataoecd/6/8/38509686.pdf*.

OECD (2008), "Gender and Sustainable Development: Maximising the Economic, Social and Environmental Role of Women", *www.oecd.org/dataoecd/58/1/40881538.pdf*.

Rollback Malaria Partnership (2008), website, accessed 5 September 2008, *www.rollbackmalaria.org*.

UN Department of Economic and Social Affairs (1993), *Agenda 21: Earth Summit – The United Nations Programme of Action from Rio*, Division for Sustainable Development, United Nations Publications, New York.

WCED (UN World Commission on Environment and Development) (1987), *Our Common Future: Report of the World Commission on Environment and Development*, WCED, Switzerland.

Chapter 3

IEA (International Energy Agency) (2007), *World Energy Outlook: China and India Insights*, OECD Publishing, Paris.

IMF (International Monetary Fund) (2006), *Ghana: Poverty Reduction Strategy Paper Annual Progress Report*, IMF Country Report 06/226, IMF, Washington, D.C.

OECD (2006), *Fishing for Coherence: Proceedings of the Workshop on Policy Coherence for Development in Fisheries*, OECD Publishing, Paris.

OECD (2005), *Trade that Benefits the Environment and Development: Opening Markets for Environmental Goods and Services*, OECD Trade Policy Studies, OECD Publishing, Paris.

OECD (2005), "Preserving Biodiversity and Promoting Biosafety", *OECD Policy Briefs*, OECD Publishing, Paris.

OECD (2005), "Paris Declaration on Aid Effectiveness", *www.oecd.org/dac/effectiveness/parisdeclaration*.

OECD (2006), *Trading Up: Economic Perspectives on Development Issues in the Multilateral Trading System*, OECD Trade Policy Studies, OECD Publishing, Paris.

OECD (2006), "Framework for Common Action around Shared Goals", adopted at the meeting of OECD Environment and Development ministers, Paris, 4 April 2006, *www.oecd.org/epocdacmin2006*.

OECD (2006), "Declaration on Integrating Climate Change Adaptation into Development Co-operation", adopted at the meeting of OECD Environment and Development ministers, Paris, 4 April 2006, *www.oecd.org/epocdacmin2006*.

OECD (2006), *Applying Strategic Environmental Assessment: Good Practice Guidance for Development Co-operation*, DAC Guidelines and Reference Series, OECD Publishing, Paris.

OECD (2007), *Development Co-operation Report 2007*, OECD Journal on Development, Vol. 9, No. 1, OECD Publishing, Paris.

OECD (2008), "Agriculture: Improving Policy Coherence for Development", *OECD Policy Briefs*, OECD Publishing, Paris.

OECD (2008), *OECD Environmental Outlook to 2030*, OECD Publishing, Paris.

OECD and WTO (World Trade Organization) (2007), "Aid for Trade at a Glance 2007", *www.oecd.org/dac/trade/aft*.

UNCTAD (United Nations Conference on Trade and Development) (2008), *Development and Globalization: Facts and Figures*, United Nations, New York.

UNDP (United Nations Development Programme) (2000), *Millenium Development Goals*, United Nations, adopted at the UN Millenium Summit, New York, 6-8 September 2000.

UNDP (2007), *Human Development Report 2007/2008: Fighting Climate Change: Human Solidarity in a divided world*, Palgrave Macmillan, New York.

UNDP (2008), "MDG Monitor: Tracking the Millennium Development Goals", *www.mdgmonitor.org/goal1.cfm*, website accessed 5 September 2008.

Chapter 4

Bates, B.C., Z.W. Kundzewicz, S. Wu and J.P. Palutikof, Eds. (2008), "Climate Change and Water", technical paper of the Intergovernmental Panel on Climate Change, IPCC Secretariat, Geneva.

FAO (Food and Agriculture Organization) (2008), *UN FAO Fishstat database*, Capture Production 1960-2006 dataset, accessed 3 September 2008, *www.fao.org/fi/statist/FISOFT/FISHPLUS.asp*.

G8 (2005), "The Gleneagles Communiqué: Climate Change, Energy and Sustainable Development", G8 Gleneagles 2005, *www.g8.utoronto.ca/summit/2005gleneagles/communique.pdf*.

Gurría, A. (2007), "The Economics of Climate Change: The Fierce Urgency of Now", speech at the UN Climate Change Conference, Bali, 12 December 2007.

IEA (2008), *Energy Technology Perspectives 2008: Scenarios and Strategies to 2050*, OECD Publishing, Paris.

Juniper Research (2008), "The 'great unbanked' to drive mobile finance market", Juniper Research, 17 June 2008, *www.juniperresearch.com.*

OECD (2006), "Good Practices in the National Sustainable Development Strategies of OECD Countries", *www.oecd.org/dataoecd/58/42/36655769.pdf.*

OECD (2008), *OECD Environmental Outlook to 2030*, OECD Publishing, Paris.

OECD (2008), "Climate Change: Meeting the Challenge to 2050", *OECD Policy Briefs*, OECD Publishing, Paris.

OECD (2008), *Teaching Sustainable Development*, OECD Publishing, Paris, forthcoming.

WCED (1987), *Our Common Future: Report of the World Commission on Environment and Development*, WCED, Switzerland.

Wray, R. (2008), "Cash in hand: why Africans are banking on the mobile phone", *The Guardian*, 17 June 2008, *www.guardian.co.uk.*

Chapter 5

Cobbing, M. (2008), "Toxic Tech: Not in our Backyard", Greenpeace International, The Netherlands, *www.greenpeace.org/raw/content/usa/press-center/reports4/toxic-tech-not-in-our-backyard.pdf.*

Nokia Corporation (2005), "Integrated Product Policy Pilot Project Stage I Final Report: Life Cycle Environmental Issues of Mobile Phones", Nokia, Ospoo, *http://ec.europa.eu/environment/ipp/pdf/nokia_mobile_05_04.pdf.*

OECD(2000), *OECD Guidelines for Multinational Enterprises, Revision 2000*, OECD Publishing, Paris.

OECD (2006), *The Political Economy of Environmentally Related Taxes*, OECD Publishing, Paris.

OECD (2008), *Measuring Sustainable Production*, OECD Sustainable Development Studies, OECD Publishing, Paris.

OECD (2008), "Promoting Sustainable Consumption: Good Practices in OECD Countries", *www.oecd.org/dataoecd/1/59/40317373.pdf.*

OECD (2008), Corporate responsibility, Directorate for Financial and Enterprise Affairs website, accessed August 2008, *www.oecd.org/daf/investment/cr.*

University of Twente, UNESCO-IHE Institute for Water Education (2008), Water footprint website, *www.waterfootprint.org*, accessed 28 August 2008.

World Resources Institute (2005), *Millennium Ecosystem Assessment: Ecosystems and Human Well-being*, Island Press, Washington, DC.

WRAP (Waste & Resources Action Programme) (2008), website, *www.wrap.org.uk*, accessed 15 August 2008.

Chapter 6

Barroso, J. M. (2007), "Beyond GDP: Opening Speech", speech at the International conference on beyond GSP: Measuring progress, true wealth and the well-being of nations, Brussels, 19 November, *www.beyond-gdp.eu/download/barroso_speech.pdf.*

Boarini, R., Å. Johansson and M. M. d'Ercole (2006), "Alternative Measures of Well-Being", *OECD Social Employment and Migration Working Papers*, No. 33, OECD Publishing, *doi:10.1787/713222332167.*

European Commission (2008), Sustainability A-Test, Sixth Framework Programme, website, *www.SustainabilityA-Test.net.*

OECD (2005), *Handbook on Constructing Composite Indicators: Methology and User Guide*, 2005 edition, OECD Publishing, Paris.

OECD (2004), *Measuring Sustainable Development: Integrated Economic, Environmental and Social Frameworks*, OECD Publishing, Paris.

OECD (2006), *Statistics, Knowledge and Policy: Key Indicators to Inform Decision Making*, OECD Publishing, Paris.

OECD (2007), *Statistics, Knowledge and Policy 2007: Measuring and Fostering the Progress of Societies*, OECD Publishing, Paris.

OECD (2008), *Conducting Sustainability Assessments*, OECD Sustainable Development Studies, OECD Publishing, Paris.

OECD (2008), *Handbook on Constructing Composite Indicators: Methodology and User Guide*, OECD Publishing, Paris.

OECD (2008), *OECD Factbook 2008: Economic, Environmental and Social Statistics*, OECD Publishing, Paris.

OECD (2008), OECD Programme on Educational Building website, *www.oecd.org/edu/facilities, accessed 2 September 2008*.

Ouroussoff, N. (2007), "Why are they greener than we are?", *New York Times Magazine*, 20 May 2007, *www.nytimes.com/2007/05/20/magazine/20europe-t.html?emc=eta1*.

Teachernet (2008), Sustainable Schools website, *www.teachernet.gov.uk/sustainableschools*, accessed August 2008.

UNECE, OECD, Eurostat Working Group on Statistics for Sustainable Development (2008), "Measuring Sustainable Development", forthcoming.

US Green Building Council (2008), website, *www.usgbc.org*, accessed August 2008.

Walker, E. (2008), "Too cool for school: Britain's most Eco-friendly building", *The Independent,* 10 April 2008, *www.independent. co.uk/environment/green-living/too-cool-for-school-britains-most-ecofriendly-building-806892.html*.

Chapter 7

BBC News (2007), "Quick Guide: Biofuels", BBC News, 25 Jan 2007, *http://news.bbc.co.uk/1/hi/sci/tech/6294133.stm*.

Dickens, C. (1850), *Oliver Twist*, Lea & Blanchard, Philadelphia.

Harrabin, R. (2008), "EU rethinks biofuels guidelines", BBC News, 14 Jan 2008, *http://news.bbc.co.uk/1/hi/world/europe/7186380.stm*.

OECD (2003), *The Environmental Performance of Public Procurement: Issues of Policy Coherence*, OECD Publishing, Paris.

OECD (2004), "Agriculture and the Environment: Lessons Learned from a Decade of OECD Work", *www.oecd.org/dataoecd/15/28/33913449.pdf*.

OECD (2005), Environmentally Harmful Subsidies: Challenges for *Reform*, OECD Publishing, Paris.

OECD (2005), "Guiding principles for regulatory quality and performance", *www.oecd.org/dataoecd/3/51/36328053.pdf*.

OECD(2006), *Competitive Cities in the Global Economy*, OECD Territorial Reviews, OECD Publishing, Paris.

OECD (2006), *Subsidy Reform and Sustainable Development: Economic, Environmental and Social Aspects*, OECD Sustainable Development Studies, OECD Publishing, Paris.

OECD (2006), *The Political Economy of Environmentally Related Taxes*, OECD Publishing, Paris.

OECD (2007), *Agricultural Policies in OECD Countries: Monitoring and Evaluation*, OECD Publishing, Paris.

OECD (2007), "Good Practices in the National Sustainable Development Strategies of OECD Countries", *www.oecd.org/dataoecd/58/42/36655769.pdf*.

OECD (2007), *Institutionalising Sustainable Development*, OECD Sustainable Development Studies, OECD Publishing, Paris.

OECD (2007), *Subsidy Reform and Sustainable Development: Political Economy Aspects*, OECD Sustainable Development Studies, OECD Publishing, Paris.

OECD (2008), "An Economic Assessment of Biofuel Environmental Policies", *www.oecd.org/dataoecd/19/62/41007840.pdf*.

OECD (2008), *Environmental Performance of Agriculture at a Glance*, OECD Publishing, Paris.

OECD (2008), *Power to the People? Building Open and Inclusive Policy Making*, OECD Publishing, Paris, forthcoming.

Rosenthal, E. (2008), "Once a Dream Fuel, Palm Oil May Be an Eco-Nightmare", *The New York Times*, 31 Jan 2008, *www.nytimes.com/2007/01/31/business/worldbusiness/31biofuel.htm*.

Sinclair, U. (1906), *The Jungle*, Doubleday, Page & Company, New York.

Swedish Ministry of the Environment (2004), *A Swedish Strategy for Sustainable Development: Economic, Social and Environmental*, Government communications 2003/04:129, *www.sweden.gov.se/content/1/c6/02/52/75/98358436.pdf*.

UN Department of Economic and Social Affairs (1993), *Agenda 21: Earth Summit – The United Nations Programme of Action from Rio*, Division for Sustainable Development, United Nations Publications, New York.

Design: Rampazzo.

Typesetting: SG Production.

Photo Credits:

Cover illustration: © florintt – Fotolia.com;
Images; pp. 8-9 © Comstock/Corbis;
     pp. 20-21 © 2008 JupiterImages Corporation;
     pp. 36-37 © 2008 JupiterImages Corporation;
     pp. 76-77 © 2008 JupiterImages Corporation;
     pp. 98-99 © Philip J Brittan/Photographer's Choice RF/
          Gettyimages;
     pp. 114-115 © Comstock/Corbis.

OECD PUBLICATIONS, 2, rue André-Pascal, 75775 PARIS CEDEX 16
PRINTED IN FRANCE
(01 2008 12 1 P) ISBN 978-92-64-04778-5 – No. 56455 2008